SAILING TO BYZANTIUM

SAILING
TO BYZANTIUM

An Architectural Companion

OSBERT LANCASTER

Illustrated by the Author

Gambit
INCORPORATED
Boston
1969

FOR ANNE

ACKNOWLEDGMENTS

MY thanks are chiefly due, first, to Father Gervase Mathew, who kindly read all the present work in typescript, and whose comments afforded me much encouragement and, I hope, preserved me from error; and second to the Hon. Sir Steven Runciman who not only read the proofs and made several valuable suggestions, but also enabled me to redeem at least one deplorable solecism.

Among many others to whom I owe a debt of gratitude for their assistance and hospitality during the twenty odd years in which this work has been in preparation—parish priests, abbots, dons, diplomats and local officials—I should like to mention in particular Professor Xyngopoulos of the University of Salonika and Doctor Bichev of the University of Sofia who kindly took time off in order to escort me on a tour of the principal monuments in their respective cities.

CONTENTS

COLOUR PLATES

FOREWORD

EACH year sees more and more travellers descending on the shores of the Eastern Mediterranean. Of these a certain proportion come solely for the sunshine and the beaches but a majority, I think, are prepared, or in some cases eager, for cultural distraction. Hitherto this has been largely provided by the ruins of classical antiquity, temples and theatres, shaft-graves and beehive tombs, but some among them there may be who feel a certain curiosity about the innumerable Byzantine churches which every-where dot the landscape; or, excited by such celebrated masterpieces as Daphni and Hosios Loukas, which are nowadays included in most of the package tours, would wish to know more of the civilisation which produced them. It is for them, and for the occasional sun-bather who at evening is moved to walk up to the little chapel on the hillside overlooking the beach, that this book is intended.

It is undeniable that an enormous library of volumes dealing with Byzan-tine art and architecture is already available, but most of them presuppose a certain knowledge in their readers, almost all are far too large to cart around in airplanes, and in a high proportion the authors have sacrificed the pleasure of imparting information to the headier joys of learned controversy. For those who in their own country are occasional church-crawlers, perfectly capable of taking a rood-screen in their stride but liable to be knocked for six by an iconostasis, no guide, so far as I know, exists.

The need is great, for Byzantine architecture developed along quite different lines to those followed by the church-builders of northern Europe, and deprived of the old happy certainties of Norman, E.E., Dec and Perp, the amateur ecclesiologist from this country may well find himself hopelessly at sea in Orthodox lands.

Unlike Gothic, Byzantine was not a progressive architecture; Hagia Sophia, which as an example of structural daring surpasses even King's College Chapel, comes not at the end but almost at the very beginning of the story. Furthermore, in the Eastern Empire there was not one but a series of renaissances, so that plans and styles evolved at an early period are frequently revived after a lapse of centuries. Nor is the chronological problem rendered any easier by the fact that this Empire flourished for longer than any in recorded history and at one period stretched from Spain to the eastern shores of the Black Sea, from the Nile to Ravenna, and its influence further still; thus a particular technique of masonry or brick-laying, which affords a sure guide to the date of a church in Macedonia, may in Cappadocia be a no less certain indication of one several centuries removed. Later additions or rebuildings, such as lady-chapels and extended bays, which in northern lands are frequently so useful chronologically, are in the East of very rare occurrence, for so logical and complete was the plan of a Byzantine church that structural alteration or extension was virtually impossible; if expansion was regarded as necessary, an entirely new church was built alongside as was done at Hosios Loukas and Paros.

In the present work I have attempted, very briefly, to summarise the development of Byzantine architecture and to indicate the whereabouts of the various examples. I start the itinerary in Ravenna, not only because nowhere else does there exist so instructive a complex of buildings dating from the earliest period, but also because nearby Venice remains in the age of the pleasure-cruise what it has always been, the traditional gateway to the East. All the buildings illustrated or described have been visited by the author (where reference is made to a building which he knows only by repute, that fact is, I hope, made clear in the text), who holds strongly to the opinion that, with architecture as with flowers, drawings, however arbitrary, are as illustrations preferable to photographs which are frequently both unselective and misleading.

Certain notable omissions will be readily detected by the expert; these are the result either of lack of first-hand knowledge or of a personal opinion that the works in question do not properly qualify as Byzantine. In the first category are the rock churches of Cappadocia, the cathedral at Trebizond, the monastery of Sinai and the Serbian churches; in the second the domed churches of Aquitaine, and the Coptic churches of Cairo. Russian architecture is excluded on both counts. Furthermore I have, as far as possible, avoided ruins, for Byzantine architecture is, by and large, strangely unimpressive in decay. The scale is usually too small and the vertical emphasis, upon which so many Gothic ruins depend for their effect, is lacking.

While I have, I hope, dealt with all the better-known masterpieces I have also made a point of including as many as possible of the small village churches, particularly in Greece and Cyprus, in the neighbourhood of which the average traveller is likely from time to time to find himself. Many of these lie on the direct route to great classical sites, or just off the road, and after a surfeit of Doric colonnades and Ionic theatres a brief visit may well provide a restful and agreeable contrast. Always small and usually decayed, the wall-paintings green-veined with damp, the plaster dropping from the Pantokrator in the dome, the Holy Table bare save for a yellowing copy of last year's 'Kathimerini' and a jam-jar half full of oil and dead flies, they are infinitely far removed from the pomp and glitter of S. Vitale or Hagia Sophia. Nevertheless at high noon, when the silence is broken only by the buzzing of the wild bees which have nested on top of the iconostasis, and the air is heavy with the smell of honey-wax candles and the wild thyme on the threshold, it is in such humble shrines as these that one may, perhaps, come closest to understanding the message of Orthodoxy. Anyhow, even a brief visit often affords an experience which the sensitive traveller would not wish knowingly to forego.

1

A PERSPECTIVE

WHEN, in A.D. 312, the Emperor Constantine was accorded such spectacular encouragement at the battle of the Milvian Bridge, the advantages, both for the Empire and the Church, which resulted from his prompt reaction, were incalculable. The Emperor, if he could no longer pretend to those divine honours which had afforded so inadequate a protection to the majority of his predecessors, was now firmly established as Christ's Vice-Regent on earth, the equal of the Apostles, and assured of the loyal support of the best organised and most powerful body among his subjects. The Church was not only relieved of all fear of further persecution but at once achieved almost unlimited influence in affairs of state and an enormous increase in revenue. For these advantages the fact that in addition to its proselytising function it would now have to act as public relations officer for the canonised Emperor seemed, at the time, a not un-reasonable *quid pro quo*.

Before the Edict of Milan (A.D. 313) places of Christian worship were plentiful but discreet; the Faithful had been accustomed to gather together in a room set aside for the purpose in one of the large blocks of flats (*insulae*) common in all the larger cities, usually on an upper floor (cf. Acts xx, 9) or occasionally in the catacombs. Now all was changed. Discretion, so far from being advisable, was disloyal; an institution so closely identified with the Imperial glory had need of buildings as sumptuous and spectacular as possible, and a whole new architecture had speedily to be developed.

To take over the temples of a demoted, but not defunct, paganism would, at this early stage, even with the imperial blessing, have been unduly pro-vocative and attended, moreover, with the risk of prolonging by association the ancient loyalties. Some entirely new type of shrine, readily distinguishable stylistically from those of rival cults, was obviously called for; the model chosen was the secular basilica, an aisled oblong hall with clerestory lighting which, from the earliest days of the Empire, had been the common form for places of public assembly, law-courts and the audience chambers in the Imperial palaces.[1] The entrance was normally, although not invariably, on the longitudinal axis with, at the opposite end, a projecting apse where stood, on a raised dais backed by a semi-circle of tiered seats, the magistrate's chair or the Emperor's throne. The adaptation of such a building for Christian Worship called for few changes; the Holy Table, free-standing, was placed in front of what now became the Bishop's throne, attendant clergy were

accommodated on the tiered seats, a covered porch or vestibule, the narthex, was added to the entrance for the Catechumens who could not, until baptised, enter the main body of the church. Baptism itself, which was still by total immersion, was carried out in a separate building, usually circular or octagonal in plan.

Such were the majority of the earliest basilicas both in Rome (S. Sabina, S. Maria Maggiore) and in the new capital Byzantium (S. John Studion). But in certain instances their simple plan had to be modified to suit exceptional conditions.

---

[1] The Christians were not, in fact, the first to realise the advantages of the basilica. That extraordinary building, the so-called 'Red Basilica' at Pergamon, although very soon transformed into a church, had originally been constructed to serve the worship of Serapis.

Even before the Peace of the Church an extensive cult of martyrs had everywhere developed; new tombs and places of martyrdom acquired an increased sanctity, and attracted the devotion of large numbers of pilgrims. Such hallowed sites were usually enclosed in small, circular or cruciform pavilions deriving their form from the far larger and more elaborate sepulchral monuments to be found along the Via Appia and other roads on the outskirts of Rome. These had now to be housed in some of the new churches.

The principal of these in Rome was naturally the tomb of St. Peter on the Vatican Hill, around which Constantine proceeded to erect the largest and the most sumptuous of all basilicas. Space was essential, not only to accommodate enormous numbers of living pilgrims but also to gratify the desire of many of the richer and more prominent members of the Christian community to be buried as close to the Apostle as possible. The main body of the new building was flanked by additional aisles making five in all, and terminated to the West (for S. Peter's was, and still is, occidented not orientated) in a large hall running at right angles to the main axis at the full height of the nave, from which it was separated by a triumphal arch, forming what was virtually a transept. Beyond this projected an apse of exceptional size, and immediately in front of it, beneath the crossing, protected by a baldacchino, lay the tomb itself.

In certain cases no attempt was made to adapt the Martyrium to the basilical plan; the central structure was simply enclosed by an ambulatory, as at S. Costanza in Rome, or provided with additional arms in the form of a cross, as in Constantine's Apostoleion (afterwards the Church of the Holy Apostles) in Constantinople. Such centralised places of worship were to exercise an important influence on the subsequent development of Byzantine church-building.

In the course of time the basilicas themselves acquired new and more elaborate features. Galleries were frequently superimposed on the side aisles which now sprouted their own apses projecting externally to the East. Exonarthexes were added to the original porch and were occasionally flanked by towers. Most important of all, transepts became increasingly common. Not only did the crossing which they formed with the nave provide a useful focal point, regardless of whether or not it marked the presence of a holy spot, but by introducing an additional bay between transept and apse the plan of the church could be made to conform to the shape of the cross. When most churches were roofed with wood the covering of this intersection presented

no particular difficulties, but as soon as timber was replaced by stone a problem arose to which Latins and Greeks found differing solutions, and it is, more than anything else, to the latter's preference for the dome (combined with the barrel vault) rather than for the cross vault, that Byzantine architecture owes its particular character.

No subject since the Procession of the Paraclete has given rise to such prolonged and embittered controversy as the origin of the dome. The honour of its invention has, at one time or another, been claimed by the embattled experts for the Romans, for the Hellenistic Greeks, for the Persians and for the Armenians; but before expressing an opinion it would be as well to consider the structural problem involved.

To place a dome on a circular building presents no great difficulty and had been achieved centuries before, the classic example being the Pantheon in Rome, but to cover a square space, such as a crossing, with a dome was a very different matter. The pragmatic solution, long common in the East, was to

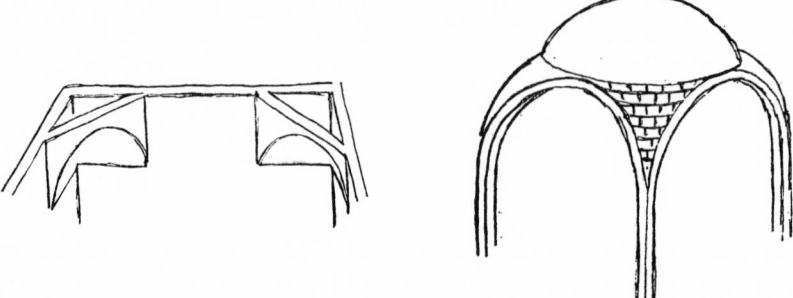

reduce the square to an octagon by placing beams, or, in stone or brick construction, arches, across the corners and by repeating the process to achieve an approximate circle. It is from the multiplication of these supporting arches, known as squinches, that the characteristic honey-comb decoration of so many Islamic buildings derives. It worked perfectly satisfactorily, but by comparison with the true dome always retained a faint suggestion of the makeshift. The true dome was finally achieved by raising arches above the sides of the square with a circle resting on their four summits, supported at the corners by brick or masonry triangles on a curved section, known as pendentives.

Who hit first on this brilliant solution, and where and when, still remains a matter for the keenest dispute. Some hold that the honour must go to the Romans, arguing that their knowledge of working in concrete and experience of roofing the vast areas of the Imperial Baths would naturally have led them to develop the pendentive. Unfortunately the only two examples which exist are both small, late and situated in the near East; the so-called Tetrahedron at Latakia (a square pavilion which once formed the corner of an arcade) and a small Roman tomb in a cemetery in Samaria. Incidentally the keen reader should be warned that neither 'vaut le detour'. Moreover, concrete is heavy, the Roman variety particularly so, and to erect even a moderate sized dome would involve very extensive buttressing.

Others hold that the pendentive derived naturally from the squinch, probably in Sassanian Persia, but as they represent fundamentally different approaches to the problem it is not, in the absence of connecting links, easy to see exactly how the transition was achieved. Others again maintain that the credit must go to the Armenians, but this involves the acceptance of dates for the earliest churches which many would dispute.

All things considered it would seem most probable that both the dome and the Byzantine style were evolved in some large Hellenistic centre of population, the geographical situation of which exposed builders and architects to the widest possible range of influences. Alexandria, Antioch and Ephesus have all at one time or another been put forward but personally I incline towards Professor Seyrig's suggestion of the great city of Seleucia-on-the-Tigris, which fulfils all the required conditions. Moreover, this theory has the additional advantage of being quite incapable of proof as not one stone remains upon another.

The development of the dome not only marked the structural divergence between Eastern and Western Christendom but may well, by reinforcing the centralising tendency of Greek worship, have encouraged liturgical differences. Long before the Great Schism, apart from such knotty problems as the use of unleavened bread, the celibacy of the clergy and the Filioque clause, Greeks and Latins were drifting apart, notably in their attitude to the Eucharist. The Mass was a sacrifice in which all present were involved; the Divine Liturgy was a sacred drama constantly re-enacted in which audience participation was not, in any physical sense, required or desirable. In the West the congregation was of major importance and the western arm of the cross was extended to accommodate them. Not only had they a right to be present but a right to see what was going on. A right, moreover, of which they were tenacious; it is recorded that in at least one mediaeval London parish disgruntled members of the congregation at the extreme west end of the church did not hesitate, at the moment of the Elevation, to interrupt the service with cries of 'Heave Him up higher!' In the East such a state of affairs was inconceivable. Here not only did the clergy annex most of the total available area but the western arm of the cross grew steadily shorter. So far from claiming their right to an uninterrupted view, Orthodox congregations accepted their total elimination from the Sacred Mysteries by a stone screen (the Iconostasis) through which the priests only occasionally appeared at certain moments during the Liturgy (the Greater and Lesser Entrances) when they entered the central area beneath the dome, of which the laity could enjoy a distant view from the narthex, aisles and galleries. The only layman who could himself participate in the service was the Emperor who, as the 13th Apostle, enjoyed semi-sacerdotal status. Hence the exceptional size of the *naos* in the great Imperial foundations. Such developments were, however, gradual and did not become systematised until the time of the Emperor Justinian from whose reign (527–65) the final establishment of a separate, clearly identifiable Byzantine culture may be said to date.

The years that had passed since the death of Constantine had not been a period of unrestricted progress. Rome itself had been sacked (A.D. 411), the Vandals had overrun North Africa, the new Empire in the East was constantly threatened by Goths, Persians and Huns from beyond the frontiers and rent internally by theological disputes of incomprehensible bitterness. For a short space Julian the Apostate had further complicated matters by a futile attempt to put back the clock, and had it not been for the great Theodosius, a Spanish general elevated to the purple in 379, there might well have been no Empire for Justinian to inherit.

Unlike almost all previous Emperors, Justinian had been in private life not a soldier but a civil servant, and his career affords, perhaps, the first great example of the truth that sometimes the memorandum is mightier than the sword. However, it seems likely that his achievement would not, for all his administrative ability, have been so great had it not been for his wife; a complex and sometimes irresolute character, subject to sudden failures of nerve, he needed exactly that stiffening and toughness which this remarkable woman was ideally fitted to provide. Theodora, who was the daughter of the man who looked after the wild bears at the Circus, had started her career on what was euphemistically described as the stage; in fact she had when young worked for a period in what was unquestionably a striptease joint. Improbable as it may seem, it was just these early experiences which made her so extraordinarily successful a consort at this particular period of history; for life in a court riddled more than most with double-crossing, back-stabbing and intrigue, a youth passed in the world of showbusiness proved an ideal preparation. Moreover, her humble origin gave her a first-hand knowledge of mob psychology just at the moment when the mobs were about to get completely out of hand.

Throughout their history the Greeks of Byzantium, at all social levels, displayed what for us must seem a wholly excessive enthusiasm for theological argument. At the time of Justinian's accession the Empire was rent by what came to be known as the Monophysite controversy, which centred round the Nature of the Incarnation. Had Our Lord two natures, divine and human, or only one, divine? And if two, did they form one substance? This question, which would seem now to be of a subtlety and complexity only to be resolved by the most highly trained dogmatic theologians, was in Byzantium eagerly debated, not only in the monasteries and at Court, but in every tavern and barber's shop in the town and nowhere more bitterly than in the Hippodrome.

One of the first great triumphs of Christian beneficence had been the suppression of those disgusting spectacles in the circus which gained for Rome a reputation for sadism which has never been successfully refuted. In Byzantium the nauseating contests between man and man and man and beast had been replaced by the healthy and exciting sport of chariot-racing, but, as other civilisations have discovered to their cost, sporting enthusiasm is apt to lead to a bitter partisanship markedly anti-social in its effects. In the Hippodrome the charioteers were divided into two teams, the Greens and the Blues, and in the fortunes of one or other every man, woman and child in the city, from the Empress to the crossing-sweepers, felt themselves personally involved. Not only did the more militant of their supporters, like the Mods and Rockers of more recent times, adopt contrasting styles of dress (the Blues, we are told, shaved the front of their heads and let their hair grow long at the back in emulation of the Huns), but constantly disturbed the peace with gang-fights on a scale which, mercifully, their 20th-century counterparts seldom, if ever, achieve. To make matters a hundred times worse, sporting passions were now exacerbated by doctrinal differences. The Greens were tinged with Monophysitism while the Blues unswervingly upheld the doctrine of the Dual Nature. For us this mingling of sport and religion normally lies beyond rational comprehension, and it is only when at Glasgow some keen supporter of Rangers rises in his seat to tell a member of the Celtic team exactly what he can do with the Pope that we may, perhaps, catch some faint echo of the normal uproar in the Byzantine Hippodrome.

In January 532 matters came to a head. The normal rivalry between Greens and Blues had been rendered more than usually embittered by some arbitrary arrests of the former's supporters. Rioting broke out, whereupon the Greens were addressed and reproached by the Emperor himself from the 'Kathisma', the Imperial Box; they responded with jeers and catcalls, thus further provoking the Blues who drove them from the Hippodrome, when the struggle continued in the streets. Very soon total anarchy prevailed, original rivalries were forgotten and both factions devoted themselves to arson and looting, crying 'Nika! Nika!' as they roamed the Capital unopposed. After five days of this the Emperor went once more to the Hippodrome hoping to quieten the mob by announcing certain concessions and pardons. However, so unwelcoming was his reception that he straightway beat a hasty retreat by the private stair back to the palace, where he succumbed to one of those sudden nervous collapses to which he was subject. At this juncture the redoubtable Theodora intervened and by her reproaches, and with the moral support of Justinian's great general, Belisarius, stiffened the resolve of her distraught husband, who thereupon ordered out the Imperial Guard, four thousand strong, into the Hippodrome where they massacred the entire audience. Order was thus drastically restored, but the price to be paid for the week-long breakdown of the rule of law was colossal; Hagia Sophia, S. Irene, half the Palace, the Baths of Zeuxippus and many churches were in ruins, and whole sections of the city were reduced to ashes. As he surveyed the damage the Emperor may well have felt disconsolate, but he was a man for whom the grand gesture always exercised an irresistible attraction and, as he realised the opportunities which reconstruction afforded, his eye may be assumed to have lit up. In that moment Byzantine architecture came of age.

The reign of Justinian marked the final abandonment of the basilica and the triumph of the dome. Justinian had already been responsible for two highly original churches, S. Vitale in Ravenna and SS. Sergius and Bacchus in the Capital, of which the latter stands in almost the same relationship to Hagia Sophia as does St. Stephen's Walbrook to St. Paul's. Painstaking attempts have been made, chiefly by German scholars, neatly to classify all

the various church plans which were now evolved under such headings as domed basilica, cross-domed basilica, domed cruciform, quincunx, etc., etc., and laboriously to trace the development from one to another. Even if they could agree among themselves to standardise such classifications and even if the problem of dating could be satisfactorily solved, such efforts would be in vain. For Byzantine architecture, unlike Gothic, was not subject to a continuously developing process. Certain features and plans recur at widely separated intervals of time and daring experiments are not invariably followed up in their place of origin but may bear fruit at the other end of the Empire centuries later. But from now on the overwhelming importance of the dome remains constant. It could be supported on barrel vaults as at S. Irene, by a combination of barrel vaults and half-domes as at Hagia Sophia, on eight piers divided by exedra as at S. Vitale. It could even multiply itself to the number of five or more, as at S. Marco, producing an effect which recalls Sydney Smith's remark on first seeing the Brighton Pavilion: 'St. Paul's has come down to the sea and pupped.'

Structural innovations involved decorative changes of which the most noteworthy are those observable in the altered form of the capital. Hitherto the types of capital favoured by the Byzantines had been elaborate and highly fancy variations on the late classical composite which have been listed under such names as the wind-blown Acanthus and the Theodosian (despite the fact that the latter had absolutely no connection with the Emperor of that name), but quite early on the actual form of the capital had to be modified to meet structural demands. The Romans had only infrequently used round-headed arches in combination with free-standing columns (as opposed to piers) and seldom, if ever, in continuous arcades.[1] In the earliest basilicas (S. Maria Maggiore for instance) the columns dividing naves and aisles supported a flat architrave, but from the 4th century on round arches became increasingly frequent and an awkward problem arose in consequence. With an architrave the weight is evenly distributed, but with an arch it is concentrated in a double thrust on the centre of the capital, and in order to

[1] The earliest surviving example of the Roman employment of arcades on a large scale is afforded by the ruins of Diocletian's palace at Split.

14

counter this and to avoid the danger of splitting, it was necessary to enlarge the supporting area. This was done by inserting a trapezoidal block of stone between the capital and the base of the arch, which is sometimes called a dosseret, sometimes a pulvino, but is most conveniently described as an impost-block. In the course of time the impost-block and the capital became structurally one and in the 6th century all attempts to distinguish between them decoratively was abandoned. In many cases only vestigial volutes, either at the top or bottom, provide any indication of classical origins, and the acanthus leaves have become areas of flat, lace-like decoration in white on black, an effect that was obtained by deep drilling. By and large the decoration remained abstract, and Byzantine craftsmen seem to have been quite unaffected by that northern 'animal-style' which in Romanesque churches produced capitals enlivened with self-devouring monsters, birds, human figures and even, at Aurillac, elephants' heads.

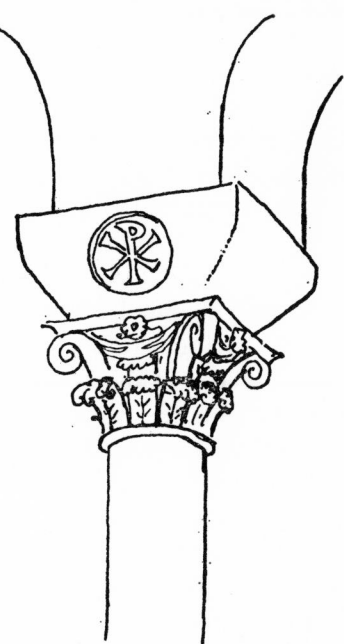

Under Justinian the Eastern Empire achieved its fullest expansion; thanks largely to the military genius of Belisarius, Rome and most of Italy were restored to the Imperial rule, the Vandals were driven out of North Africa, and the North Eastern frontiers were firmly established on the Danube. After Justinian's death a gradual decline set in that was much accelerated in the following century by the emergence of the Arabs who, within less than a century of Mahomet's death, had permanently relieved the Empire of Syria, Egypt and North Africa and had extended their sway to Persia and Spain. On two occasions they even reached the outskirts of the Capital and the city was only saved by its magnificent walls and the skilful employment of the great Byzantine secret weapon, Greek fire. In the next century disintegration was temporarily halted by the Isaurian Emperors, but it was not until the emergence of the Macedonian dynasty in 867 that a new period of stability and achievement was finally established.

It was not, however, external disasters so much as internal disputes which during this period so powerfully interfered with progress of the arts. In 717 the Imperial throne was occupied by a tough soldier from the borders of Syria, Leo the Isaurian, whose religious position was, to borrow an Anglican term of reference, considerably Lower than the angels. In his view all representation of sacred personages provided a direct encouragement to idolatry and he immediately launched a campaign of image-breaking of a ruthless thoroughness unsurpassed even by Cromwell. How far his religious convictions were reinforced by a possible Semitic origin, or encouraged by the example of Islam, remain matters for dispute; what is in no sort of doubt was the strength of the reaction they provoked. The Iconodules, as the supporters of images were called, rose in defence of the Holy Pictures headed by the monks, who in the Orthodox Church were a far more turbulent element than they ever were in the West. Persecution on a wide scale followed, and was intensified in the reign of Leo's son, Constantine Copronymos, and the Iconodules could soon boast a number of martyrs of whom the most memorable was, perhaps, a strong-minded lady named Theodosia who did not hesitate to pull a ladder from under a soldier who, on the Emperor's instructions, was demolishing the great Icon of Christ above the main gateway of the Imperial Palace. As a result the man broke his neck, whereupon his companions rushed Theodosia to the Hippodrome and summarily dispatched her by driving a ram's horn through her throat.

The effects of the Iconoclastic controversy, which raged on and off for a century or more, were widespread and lasting. Thanks to the zeal of the Iconoclasts no paintings or mosaics of the first great period of Byzantine art exist in Constantinople today—even the portrait of Justinian in the narthex of Hagia Sophia is a 9th-century replacement—and for these we must look to Ravenna, where destruction was averted by the fact that it had long since passed over to the Western obedience which remained staunchly iconodule. Large numbers of artists and craftsmen emigrated; some to Rome, where their influence is clearly detectable in many 8th- and 9th-century churches, some to Damascus and Jerusalem, where they found employment with the cultivated dynasty of the Ommayads. But in the long run it was the final settlement of the dispute, largely in favour of the Iconodules, which, by defining at considerable length the Orthodox Church's attitude towards the cult of images, exercised the most profound influence, not only on the painting, but also indirectly on the architecture, in the years to come.

The principal argument of the Iconoclasts had been based on the proposition that correctly to portray the Godhead was impossible and that any attempt to do so must of necessity be blasphemous and heretical. This view

16

was now itself defined as heresy on the ground that, as Our Lord had taken upon Himself human form, to maintain that He could not be represented pictorially was to deny the Incarnation. However, in order to guard against human error the exact manner in which Our Lord, or any sacred personage, was to be portrayed was defined with the greatest exactness in accordance with Christological and Neo-Platonic theories governing the exact relationship between Image and Reality as laid down by such authorities as John of Studion and St. John Damascene.

Superficially, certain of the paintings in a Romanesque church may seem to resemble those we find in Byzantine churches of this date, but the artists were, in fact, pursuing totally different objectives. The former are didactic, the latter sacramental. The scenes and characters in such a church as S. Savin, for instance, are there, apart from fulfilling a decorative function, to familiarise the unlettered faithful with the scenes and personages of Holy Writ; at Hosios Loukas or Daphni they exist in their own right as participants in the Divine Liturgy, affording the worshipper not instruction but an opportunity for veneration.

Thus the complete disinterest in pictorial space which characterises so much Byzantine painting springs not from incompetence or lack of curiosity but is a calculated rejection; there is no need to show the Baptist, for example, carefully and realistically planted on the banks of the Jordan, which can be quite arbitrarily indicated not as a setting but as an attribute, because he is not intended to be on the banks of the Jordan but right here in this very church. The logical extension of this sacramental method of representation produced some curious theories (that may well in their origins pre-date Christianity), which had a direct effect on architecture. Thus a person was not deemed to be really present if both his eyes were not clearly visible and ideally the frontal position was preferable to all others as being the most suitable for veneration. But when it was necessary that two personages should confront one another, as in the Annunciation, this rule had to be modified and a half-profile with both eyes visible was permitted. However, even this adjustment was not always sufficient firmly to establish the connection and this led to an increased use of curved surfaces (and the revival of the squinch) which rendered possible the placing of the Virgin and the Angel at an angle to each other and to utilise the real, as opposed to the pictured space, which lay between them. The only scriptural personage who is invariably portrayed in profile is Judas Iscariot, whose real presence was naturally not required.

The attempt to systematise church decoration during the Macedonian period had a profound effect on architecture and led to the widespread adoption of the cross-in-square plan. Basically cruciform, with a dome supported on barrel vaults and the angles of the cross filled in to produce a square plan at ground level and a cross above, this arrangement was capable of considerable variation (the dome might be supported on four free-standing

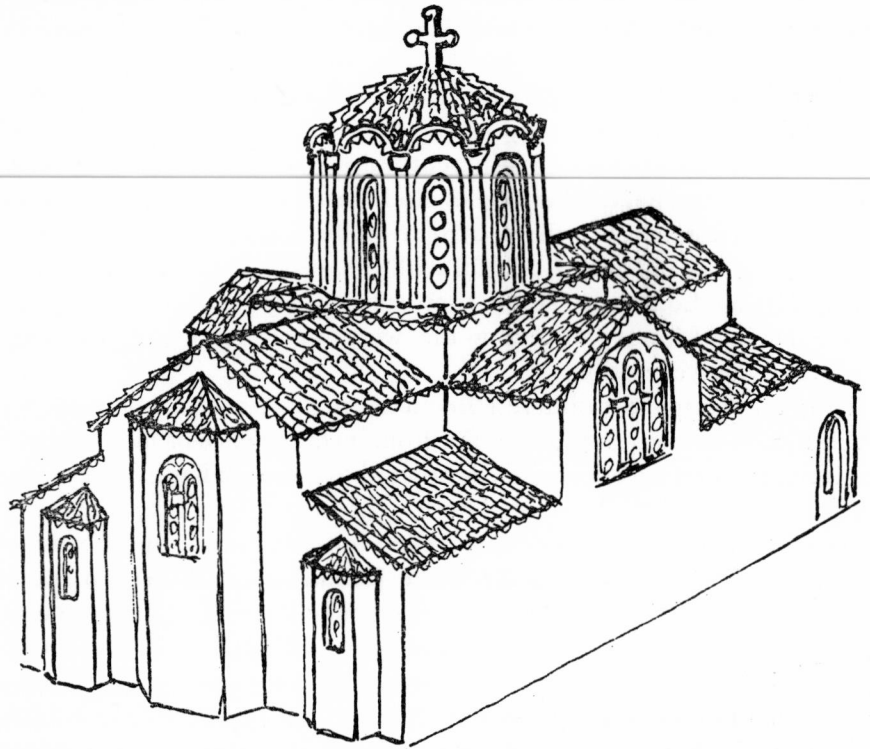

pillars, or on extensions of the piers separating the *naos* from the *bema* and narthex, or on two pillars and two piers), but remained ideally suited to the avowed purpose of the Byzantine church builders of this period which was to produce a logical working model of the cosmos. High above all, remote, all-seeing, Christ Pantokrator (Almighty) gazes down from the interior of the dome; on a slightly lower level, in the half-dome of the apse, is the Theotokos (Mother of God) flanked by archangels; in the intervening zone between heaven and earth are the apostles with the evangelists in the pendentives; just above ground level are the Fathers of the Church, the Stylites, the military saints, the martyrs, all in their appointed place; while in the apse, immediately below the Virgin, is depicted the Communion of the Apostles, symbolising the constantly renewed link between Man and God, Heaven and Earth. Scenes from the life of Our Lord, of which the Crucifixion does not, as in the West, constitute the most important, are confined to the transepts and the western bay, and scenes from the life of the Virgin to the narthex. The Doom or Judgement, which in the West, particularly in England, occupies so prominent a position above the chancel-arch, in Byzantine churches is banished either to the west wall or to the exo-narthex. The actual delineation of all these saints and their spatial relationship to each other in traditional scenes such as the Betrayal, or the Entry into Jerusalem, had been carefully worked out by higher authority and no variations inspired by the personal whim of the artist were tolerated for a moment. The Trinity was symbolised by the three angels entertained by Abraham unawares, the Anastasis (Resurrection) is represented not by the Rising from the Tomb, as in the West, but by the trampling of the Gates of Hell. The Prodromos (John the Baptist) has always to be shown very thin, clad in skins and with a tangled beard. St. Demetrios must always ride on a red horse, St. George on a white one. In the case of the latter a charmingly light-hearted touch, one of the very few in Byzantine iconography, is occasionally provided by the presence of the saint's coffee boy, very, very small, sitting up behind him.

Hitherto Byzantine architecture had been markedly introvert; that is to say that the central area covered by the dome was all-important and its relationship to the outer walls was a secondary consideration. It could be surrounded by an ambulatory or flanked with aisles, enclosed in an octagon or in a square. Least important of all was the external appearance. S. Vitale seen from without is severely functional and Hagia Sophia itself, even without the buttresses, minarets and other additions which now confuse the silhouette, must always have relied on its size alone to make an effect. Now comes a change; the external walls, particularly on the Greek mainland and the Peloponnese, are enlivened with intricate patterns in cut brick; beneath the eaves and round the apse stretch elaborate meanders inspired by the Cufic texts employed by the Arabs in similar positions in mosques, but here without any literary significance. Sculptural slabs, fragments of classical entablatures, even, on occasion, ceramic plates, are all pressed into service to produce a cloisonné effect of extreme richness. At the same time the dome is raised on a drum, which tends to get steadily higher as the years go by, particularly in the north, usually polygonal. In all probability this development arose in answer to a demand for more picture space in which the prophets could conveniently, and logically, be portrayed. Externally the dome could be roofed in a variety of ways; in Athens, but nowhere else, it is egg-shaped and its silhouette is continuous with that of the drum; elsewhere it is covered either by a shallow cone with projecting eaves, or else by a half-sphere surmounting eaves which take their shape from the line of the arcading surrounding the windows.

In the two centuries which followed the accession of Basil the Macedonian the power and the glory of the Empire remained to all appearances undimmed. Palace revolutions and the matrimonial misadventures of the last but one of the Macedonians, that ridiculous figure the Empress Zoe, the faded blonde who stares so dumbly at us in the gallery of Hagia Sophia, were not in themselves sufficient seriously to weaken the régime, and the Comnene dynasty which succeeded produced some exceptionally able rulers. The shock, therefore, when the city at last fell, not to the Arabs or the Avars or the Huns, but to the God-fearing thugs of the Fourth Crusade, was fearful. The reasons for the disaster were, in fact, twofold, economic and military. The financial position had been hopelessly undermined by the debasement of the currency by the Emperor Constantine Monomachos, and commerce was to be increasingly hamstrung by the progressive concessions made to the Venetians and Genoese business communities; and in the year 1071 the Emperor Romanos at the disastrous battle of Manzikert lost not only the hard core of the professional army, but also the Empire's main recruiting grounds, to the Seljuk Turks.

The flower of Western chivalry, who now became the Masters of the East, were a bunch of illiterate, rapacious and conscienceless toughs, hopelessly inferior in all the polite arts to the foes they vanquished. They looted, raped and smashed in the name of Christ and the Filioque clause and the only

20

appreciation they displayed of the treasures they stole sprang from a super-stitious regard for the most trivial relics. Not so the Venetians, the financial backers of the whole enterprise; no whit inferior to the Latins in avarice, they at least had a very shrewd idea of the value, both monetary and aesthetic, of what they removed.

It was not to be expected that the Latin Empire which was now set up in Constantinople would have a very long life, nor did it. In 1261, less than a hundred years after the fall, the ramshackle dominion of competing robber-barons came to its unillustrious end and the Orthodox and God-protected Emperor Michael Palaeologos returned to the great city from his makeshift capital at Nicaea.

But the Constantinople to which the Emperor came back was no longer the splendid metropolis of the Macedonians. Large areas within the walls had reverted to fields and gardens, many churches were stripped and desecrated; all the palaces were gutted or in ruins and the Treasury was empty. Only in the flourishing Genoese quarter across the Horn was there business as usual. Nevertheless, it is a surprising and gratifying fact that it was in these depressing conditions, with the Imperial frontiers annually contracting until finally they embraced little save the city itself, with distant outposts such as Mistra and Salonica isolated and threatened, that, in the comparatively few years remaining before the final disaster, Byzantine art enjoyed its last, and perhaps most astonishing, flowering.

It is only in recent years (particularly since the discoveries at the Kahriye Djami) that the achievements of the Palaeologan Revival, as it is now generally called, have been properly appreciated. Formerly, despite the evidence of Mistra, it was arbitrarily assumed that these latter-day Byzantines lacked both the means and the will to embark on even moderate sized enter-prises; that impoverishment had dictated the substitution of painting for mosaic; that such originality as the artists displayed was but a pale reflection of the artistic quickening at the other end of the Mediterranean. It is now clear that not only could they perfectly well afford the most sumptuous mosaics but retained all their old skill in the art, and it is probable that the sudden popularity of painting was due rather to the greater freedom and scope for dramatic expression which the medium afforded, and which the breakdown of the old rigid rules of the Post-Iconoclastic period permitted. As to Western influence, this was extremely limited and confined almost en-tirely to architectural details—the Pantanassa at Mistra can boast a cam-panile with pinnacles and some rather clumsy Gothic strap-work round the apse, and at Monemvasia and in Cyprus the pointed arch makes a fleeting appearance. As far as painting is concerned it seems highly probable that the wind of change was blowing in the opposite direction some years before the Greek dispersion.

Architecturally the most interesting development during the period was the elaboration and enlargement of the cross-in-square plan, with an ever-increasing richness of external decoration in brick. The number of domes was frequently increased to five, not, however, disposed as at S. Mark's or S. John at Ephesus, along the arms of the cross, but covering the spaces

enclosed in the angles, as in the Holy Apostles at Salonica. This proved particularly popular in the north and had a considerable influence on the subsequent development of Russian architecture.

So great was the shock produced by the final disaster (1453) and so dramatic the circumstances that the immediate effects of the Turkish conquest are liable to be regarded as rather more catastrophic and far-reaching than in fact, anyhow at first, they probably were. The Turks possessed all the military virtues in abundance but never then or at any time displayed the smallest talent for administration; they were forced, therefore, in order to maintain their conquest as a going concern, to take over intact a large number of Byzantine institutions with the result that the Ottoman Empire, certainly in the early days, had far more in common with the régime it displaced than is generally recognised. Not only were the Civil Service, and even many of the Grand Viziers, Greeks, but such features of life on the Golden Horn as we have come to regard as peculiarly Turkish—the eunuchs, the Janissaries, the court ritual and even the enormous, bulbous, turbans—were all flourishing under the Palaeologues.

Artistically the Ottomans had shown themselves to be rather less gifted than their predecessors, the Seljuks, and the architecture of their capital at Bursa was, with one exception—the magnificent Great Mosque—picturesque rather than imaginative, and even the Great Mosque, overwhelming as is the effect produced by the twenty domes, is, spatially, almost naïvely uninventive. It was not, therefore, surprising that, confronted with the architectural glories of their prize, the Turks should have been haunted by a feeling of inadequacy that was only finally dispelled in the reign of Suleiman the Magnificent.

The career and triumphs of the great Sinan lie well outside the scope of this book, nevertheless he must in one sense be regarded as the end product of the Byzantine architectural tradition. For he was not only one of the world's great architects but the first with the skill and appreciation to continue where Anthemios of Tralles had left off almost a millennium before. Possibly a Greek, possibly an Armenian, but certainly not a Turk, he was the one man capable of profiting by the example of Hagia Sophia and providing Islam with a comparable shrine. Thanks to him Turkish architecture at its best may be regarded, in its manipulation of space, as an extension of the Byzantine achievement.

In the realm of painting the old tradition was humbly carried on in out-of-the-way corners of the old Empire for centuries. Thus the remarkably complete series of murals at Kaisariani in Attica are dated 1672, many of the monasteries on Athos were decorated in the 18th century, and in Bulgaria icons which to all but the expert eye would appear to be of 15th- or 16th-century date were in fact produced when Queen Victoria had been on the throne for years. It was only at the very end of the century that the art of the Orthodox world was finally submerged beneath a floor of *bondieuseries*, Russian in inspiration, which for oleaginous sentimentality will stand comparison with the most fearsome products of the Place Saint Sulpice.

Most Greek churches are kept firmly locked, a precaution which, to judge by the number of icons regularly available at the dealers in London and New York, is, though belated, fully justified. However, the key is usually readily available; no matter how deserted the landscape, a small boy capable of producing it is almost certain to pop up from nowhere. Nevertheless, it is advisable, particularly in Cyprus, if the church is very isolated, to enquire for the *pappas* at the nearest village, so saving oneself a possible double trip. If the *pappas* comes himself, as he almost certainly will, a small donation is quite in order, but care should be taken to stress that it is for the *church*, otherwise feelings may be wounded. If the church is open, but totally deserted, light a five-drachma candle and put twenty drachmas in the box.

As very few churches possess artificial light, and as in most cases some of the best details are in the remotest corners, a good torch and a pair of field-glasses are essential equipment. Formerly, women were never allowed beyond the iconostasis, but nowadays this rule is not so strongly enforced, anyhow in the more sophisticated districts; nevertheless, if a *pappas* is present they should await his invitation before proceeding. If by ill-luck the guardian is a nun, any attempt by a member of her own sex to come anywhere near the sanctuary will produce an immediate explosion. No one, male or female, should on any account use the Holy Door, but should go in by one of the side openings in the screen.

As many of the most popular saints in the Orthodox church are unfamiliar in the West, a few identifying clues may be welcome, for, although they are usually labelled, the Byzantine script is not easy to decipher, even for good Greek scholars. St. George is readily recognisable, but if neither the dragon nor the princess are depicted, he can easily be mistaken for St. Demetrios; the distinction lies in the colour of their mounts, white for St. George, red for St. Demetrios. Of the military saints, the most popular are the Two Theodores, who are usually shown on foot, but may occasionally appear on horse-back, riding side by side like Castor and Pollux. An elderly bishop wearing an extraordinary basket-work hat is St. Spyridon, the patron saint of Corfu, who is frequently shown waving the burning tile with which he rather speciously demonstrated the con-substantiality of the Holy Trinity at the Council of Nicaea. The head and shoulders of an old gentleman in a pixie hood mounted on the top of a column is St. Simeon Stylites or one of his companions. A withered hag, naked except for her long white hair, is St. Mary of Egypt, and an equally naked old man with a long, concealing beard is St. Onofrios. St. Mammas, the patron saint of tax-payers, is invariably depicted astride the lion with which he frightened the daylights out of the Cypriot inland revenue, and the Emperor Constantine and his Mother St. Helena are usually shown together, crowned, and in full court dress, on either side of the Cross. A crowd of naked soldiers huddled together in a pond are the Forty Martyrs of Sebaste, and a bishop with a dachshund's head is St. Christophoros Cynocephalos, and one holding a money bag is St. John the Almoner. In the north of Greece one sometimes comes across icons and paintings, rather late in date, of haloed figures wearing the fustanella and red, Albanian fez; these are local saints martyred by the Turks.

2

THE WESTERN MARCHES

EVEN among the last, shadowy Roman Emperors Honorius was conspicuously dim. Indolent, cowardly and indecisive, Gibbon denies him every manly virtue and only qualifies the charge of impotence in order to suggest that his affection for his sister may, perhaps, have passed beyond the bounds of brotherly love. Nevertheless, few men can ever have had so highly developed a sense of self-preservation, for in an era of unsurpassed turbulence he not only succeeded in remaining on his throne for a far longer period than had all but a few of his predecessors, but died in his bed. Never did this instinct serve him better than when it prompted the choice of site for his new capital.

By the beginning of the 5th century Milan had become uncomfortably exposed to barbarian inroads, and Honorius, after several unfortunate experiences, very wisely transferred himself and his court to Ravenna. The chief, indeed the only, advantage possessed by the town, which was small and undistinguished, was its geographical position. Three miles upstream from the great Imperial naval base of Classe, on the most southerly mouth of the Po, its sea communications with what remained of the Western Empire and, far more important, with Constantinople, were assured, while on the landward side a wide complex of streams, marshes and lagoons afforded sure protection from roving bands of Goths or Lombards.

It is not, however, to Honorius that the credit for the expansion and embellishment of the new Capital chiefly belongs but to his sister, Galla Placidia. This remarkable woman, the only one of Theodosius' children to inherit something of their father's character, had, after a childhood spent in Constantinople, accompanied her brother to the West, and was living in Rome at the time of the sack, which he prudently was not. Taken captive by the Goths she was moved to southern Gaul and, after much unpleasantness, given in marriage to Adolphus, the brother-in-law of King Alaric with whom Honorius had come to terms. On his death she returned to Ravenna where she married a general, Constantius by name, who did not long survive, by whom she had a son, and, with the title of Augusta, became the effective, if not the nominal, ruler of the West. On the death of Honorius in 423 she was forced temporarily to take refuge with her nephew, Theodosius II, the Emperor of the East, but was soon back in Ravenna where she continued to reign in the name of her infant son, who had been proclaimed Honorius' successor with the title of Valentinian III, until her death in 450.

As sole Emperor, Valentinian did not prove a success and after a period of considerable confusion Ravenna fell to Theodoric, King of the Ostrogoths, allegedly acting on behalf of the Eastern Emperor, Zeno. This Wagnerian figure, although totally illiterate and a heretic, was not unappreciative of the architectural glories of his new acquisition, which he immediately decided to emulate, sending all over Italy for marbles, columns and building materials, and his long reign constitutes the second great period in Ravenna's architectural history.

Even had Theodoric's successors proved less incompetent than they did, it is doubtful whether the Gothic régime at Ravenna could long have survived. With the accession of Justinian the Greeks were launched on an expansionist policy directed at restoring the Western Empire to the rule of Constantinople, a policy which, thanks to the military abilities of Belisarius and Narses, was at length successfully carried out. After the former's capture of Rome in 536, Ravenna passed almost without a struggle into Byzantine hands. To mark the importance which he attached to the new conquest, Justinian, who did not go so far as to visit it himself, made it the seat of an Exarch through whom he hoped to control all Italy, and embarked on a big building programme by remote, but strict, control.

Few of Justinian's successors displayed any very keen interest in Ravenna, still fewer were in any position to further it if they did, and with the break-up of the West the city soon became a lonely outpost of the Empire, a Byzantine prestige symbol just maintainable so long as Constantinople controlled the sea-lanes. Unfortunately, as the centuries passed, the sea itself withdrew leaving the city, magnificent and remote, isolated from the outside world by gloomy pine-forests and dismal marshes. In such circumstances it was not to be expected that the inhabitants would continue the great architectural tradition of their former rulers and it says much for their patriotism and their energy that they were able to maintain what they had inherited.

This was no easy task, for the continuous retreat of the sea led to a constant rise in the ground-level, and practically every old building in the city shows signs of frequent reconstruction intended to offset the aesthetic disadvantages this process produced.

With Ravenna inaccessible to all boats save those of the shallowest draught, trade naturally moved elsewhere, and from the 7th century onwards it was the islands at the head of the Adriatic, on which refugees from the constantly threatened mainland had recently established themselves, which maintained and developed commercial contacts with the East. Of these Venice soon became the most important and remained for five hundred years the principal link between East and West. Not only was there a permanent Venetian trade-mission in Constantinople but for centuries there flourished a prosperous Greek-speaking colony in Venice, whose former presence is commemorated by the church of S. Giorgio dei Greci. The architectural end-product of this relationship is today the largest and most magnificent of all Byzantine churches still functioning as a place of Christian worship, the cathedral of S. Mark.

RAVENNA

The Baptistry of the Orthodox. This is the only building in Ravenna of which the foundation pre-dates the arrival of Galla Placidia. However, although work probably started as early as A.D. 400, decoration, and some structural elaboration, continued as late as 450. Octagonal in plan and severely plain externally, it used to be thought, heaven knows why, that it was part of an old Roman bath. The interior as it exists today is one of the most extraordinary phenomena in the whole history of Western architecture.

In the centre of the dome is a circular mosaic of the Baptism in Jordan with, prominent in the foreground, the titular deity of the river, damp and hirsute. (Of all the old classic pantheon the local river-gods were to prove the most long-lived.) Surrounding this is a procession of the apostles briskly advancing with a wonderful, rhythmic liveliness, bearing crowns in veiled hands. Below this are eight mosaic panels, divided by extraordinary formalised plant-forms, in each of which is depicted the empty throne awaiting the Second Coming set in a perspective architectural niche which may possibly derive directly from late Roman stage-settings and ultimately from Pompeian wall-paintings. Below each of these panels is a round-headed window flanked by small, three-dimensional marble arcades with variously shaped pediments, each enclosing a toga-ed, and presumably sacred, personage, and surmounted by pairs of confronted animals of a playfulness that is almost arch.

Immediately above, enclosing both window and arcades, is a semi-circular lunette decorated very light-heartedly with vases and foliage in white moulded stucco on a coloured ground. At floor-level, or rather what is now floor-level, are more lunettes surmounting coloured marble revetments in geometrical patterns, decorated with gold acanthus scrolls in mosaic with figures of saints in the spandrels.

Many people, while duly admiring the incredibly beautiful procession of apostles, find this astonishing mixture of Palaeo-Christian, late classical *hommes-en-arcades*, straight Byzantine and Oliver Messel rococo confusing, distasteful and possibly faux-naïf. Personally I like it very much.

The Mausoleum of Galla Placidia. Somewhere around 425 Galla Placidia built a church to which was attached a mausoleum intended for herself and her brother. Of the church all but a battered and much altered nave has

vanished, but mercifully, and almost miraculously, the mausoleum has survived intact. It is a small cruciform building with barrel-vaulted arms and a crossing surmounted by a dome on pendentives constructed, not of brick or stone, but of interlocking terra-cotta amphorae, an ingenious contemporary device very popular on account of its lightness. The exterior relieved only by blind arcading and classical cornices, is markedly austere, in sharp contrast to what lies within.

Once one's eyes have become accustomed to the gloom, for the thin, semi-transparent alabaster slabs which have recently, and quite correctly, been put back in the few small windows severely ration the light, one is over-whelmed by the richness of the decoration. The barrel vaults are covered with a pattern of rosettes and stars on a blue ground of an intensity which, in all their long history, Byzantine mosaicists never again achieved. In the arches beneath the dome are four pairs of confronted apostles; lower down deer graze amidst a tangle of golden acanthus tendrils. All the returns and soffits are enriched with bands and borders of abstract decoration in red, blue, green and gold, and here and there pairs of doves are decoratively posed on ornamental fountains.

If, after a short while, the visitor finds the total effect a little overpowering he should remember that in the course of time the floor-level has risen con-siderably, some say by as much as five feet, and that originally the star-encrusted dome would have been further above his head than it is today.

One advantage of this involuntary elevation, however, is that one is now in an ideal position to study the two fascinating panels in the lunettes to west and east. Over the door is the Good Shepherd, a beardless Christ seated on a mound and holding a cross, surrounded by sheep and portrayed in a late classical style, almost impressionist in its technique. Opposite, St. Lawrence hurries towards the gridiron, spouting formalised flames, which separates him from a small bookcase containing the Gospels, all neatly labelled, the whole conceived and carried out with a literalism and attention to detail that leaves no room for correct perspective or delicate atmospheric effects. (Incidentally, this is the first example in Christian art of anyone other than Our Lord being adorned with a halo.)

Immediately beneath this lunette stands an enormous sarcophagus that once contained the body of Galla Placidia but is now, alas, empty. Once long ago, so the story goes, some children playing in the mausoleum espied through a crack in the sarcophagus the faint glitter of a golden shroud. In order to see more clearly they pushed in a lighted taper, with the result that after a thousand years all that was mortal of this remarkable princess went up in smoke.

As one stands beneath this first of Christian domes, flanked by those two so remarkably contrasted panels, one has a strong feeling that here beneath one's feet runs the line dividing the old classical world from the age of Faith.

Replace the cross by a lyre and the Good Shepherd immediately becomes Orpheus charming the animals, or Apollo himself. To St. Lawrence, on the other hand, there attaches no hint of the Hellenistic past; haloed and single-minded, he is the first of a long line of jaunty, mediaeval martyrs, the fore-runner of a style in which attributes were to be far more important than atmosphere.

S. Giovanni Evangelistra. This church, built originally between 424 and 434 by Galla Placidia by way of thank-offering for her rescue from shipwreck, has undergone many alterations due to natural causes and enemy action. The final recon-struction carried out after the bombardment in World War II was extensive but tactful. In plan the church is a straightforward basilica of which the only specifically Byzantine features are the apse, which is polygonal on the outside, not semi-circular as was usual in Rome, and the use of impost-blocks above the handsome late classical capitals in the nave. The pillars and the aisle arcade itself were first raised in the 7th century and the original pavement is today more than six feet below ground-level. The three lower windows in the apse have been bricked up and light now comes from above through seven round-headed windows con-
nected in a continuous arcade which, it is suggested, was part of the original structure. If this is so, then the three lower windows must be later addi-tions, for they could not possibly on structural, as well as aesthetic, grounds have co-existed. The aisles do not terminate internally in apses, but on the outside are two free-standing square chambers, the exact purpose of which has given rise to much speculation.

The base of the 11th-century campanile is visible on the south side of what was the narthex and may possibly rest on the foundations of one of a pair of flanking towers. Propped against the side walls are a series of 'mosaic' panels recounting some complicated military exploit in the style of a primitive strip-cartoon, of uncertain date but unquestioned ineptitude.[1] Outside the

[1] Quite possibly the capture of Constantinople by the Fourth Crusade as seen through Western eyes.

west entrance is a large almost entirely rebuilt forecourt which may occupy the site of the original *atrium*. Despite the bombing it still retains an elaborate *trecento* portico which reinforces one's belief that Gothic was a style which the Italians were on the whole well advised to neglect.

The Baptistry of the Arians. This was built by Theodoric on behalf of his co-religionists as a direct challenge to that of the Orthodox, the structure and decoration of which it follows closely. Equally uninspiring outside, the interior fails to provide the same compensating pleasures. All that is left above the bare brick of the walls is the Baptism in the dome and the surrounding ring of apostles. The latter are, admittedly, far inferior to those in the Orthodox Baptistry—all the bounce and movement have gone—but the former is, I think, rather unjustly decried. Undoubtedly much coarser in technique, it nevertheless displays a primitive, Sunday-painter directness which, in my view, just enables it to hold its own with its more sophisticated counterpart.

The Tomb of Theodoric. One glance at this massive and unattractive mausoleum is sufficient to dispel all doubts about the racial origins of its creator, and at once transforms the pleasant little park in which it stands into some corner of a foreign field which is for ever Deutschland. Built about 526, it contains a cruciform tomb-chamber at ground-level surmounted by a circular apartment, crowned with a shallow dome made from a single gigantic slab of marble and formerly surrounded by a gallery. The most unusual feature of the building is the material of its construction, for in the West stone had by this date long since given way to brick. Perhaps this archaism was due to some subconscious memory of all those ancestral barbarian tumuli closed with a single slab of moorland granite; perhaps it sprang from a conscious desire to emulate the glories of imperial Rome. Anyhow, as it stands today, the building produces an extraordinary illusion of having been transported intact from late 19th-century Munich—an illusion much strengthened by the faint suggestion of *Jugendstil* conveyed by the square lugs, presumably functional in origin, still fringing the edge of the dome.

Mercifully this monstrous structure had no influence whatever on the subsequent development of Byzantine architecture.

S. Apollinare Nuovo. Of all the churches built by Theodoric this is the only one remaining in anything approaching its original condition. A straightforward, rather narrow, basilica terminating in a half-domed apse, the plan is unremarkable and it is to the remaining mosaics (those in the apse have vanished) that it owes its fame. These are laid out in three parallel zones running the whole length of the nave. The topmost consists of panels depicting scenes from the life of Our Lord in that almost *fauve* style employed on a similarly situated series in S. Maria Maggiore in Rome. Doubtless as manuscript illuminations, to which in all probability they owe their inspiration, they would be effective enough, but in their actual position, above the windows and against the light, their pictorial value is almost nil and their decorative function slight. Below them, and between the windows, are figures of saints, rather out-of-scale with the space they occupy and, I suspect, much restored. However, all tendency to carp is immediately banished by the sight of the lowest zone, immediately above the arcades. On the north a wonderful procession of Virgin Martyrs, dressed in green and gold and separated by formalised palm trees, advance from the port of Classe bearing their crowns towards the Virgin and Child between angels. At the head of the column are the three Magi presenting their gifts with a hurried eagerness in marked contrast to the grave rhythm of their followers. Opposite, on the south, a long line of male saints, equally stately, are leaving Theodoric's palace at Ravenna and advancing towards their Saviour.

Exquisitely beautiful as are these two long panels, they pose certain questions. Why should these two processions start from Classe and Ravenna respectively, neither of which cities was particularly noted for the number of its martyrs? And why are they carried out in a markedly different style from the two charming townscapes and the remaining mosaics? It seems probable that what happened was that the saints replaced an earlier representation of Theodoric and his court, engaged on a similar errand, who would quite logically be taking off from the palace and the port; a substitution carried out by Justinian who had no wish at all to prolong the memory of his Arian predecessor. In which case it is possible that the Magi, who are so noticeably out-of-step, may also belong to the earlier series. Anyhow, they were heavily restored in the 19th century, when the crowns with which they were at that time adorned were replaced, probably quite correctly, by the Phrygian caps they wear today.

On the west wall of the church there is a small portrait mosaic of Justinian, coarse in workmanship and of doubtful authenticity.

S. Vitale. Before entering the church the visitor must brace himself to face the 18th century, during which period all the existing painted decoration was carried out. While a Gothic church possesses an organic quality which allows it to absorb the imposition, within reason, of subsequent styles (the Jacobean tomb is accommodated without difficulty beneath the E.E. arches, the Victorian glass fits quite snugly into the perpendicular tracery), the Byzantine church, which is by no means organic, but a finite, intellectual concept fixed for ever in one particular moment of time, does not. Thus any stylistic deviation has an immediately disruptive visual impact for which it is as well to be prepared in advance. Not that these paintings are in themselves despicable: given the conventions of the time they are remarkably tactful; but the contrast between the austere, hieratic angels in the apse and the airborne putti cavorting round the dome is likely to prove rather too violent for those coming upon it unawares.

That S. Vitale was built early in the reign of Justinian (nominally by Archbishop Ecclesius) is certain, but about the exact date there is much controversy. Normally this would be of small importance, but in this case great interest, at least for architectural historians, attaches to the question whether it is earlier or later than or contemporary with either Hagia Sophia or SS. Sergius and Bacchus in Constantinople, with both of which churches it has novel features in common. In default of any written evidence, which is extremely unlikely to turn up, we shall never know, but my own guess, for what it is worth, is that the plans had left the drawing-board before work had started on the former but after the completion of the latter.

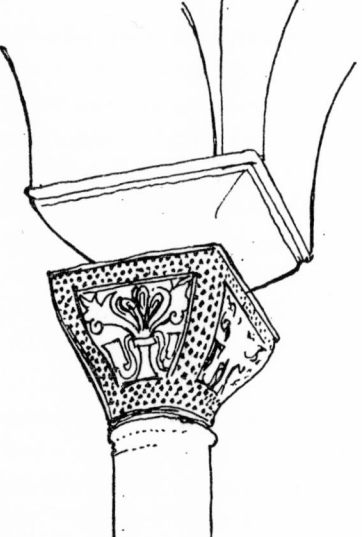

The plan, although it probably derives ultimately from earlier baptistries or martyria, is markedly original. Eight piers are separated by seven exedra and a short presbytery ending in an apse. This octagon is reduced to a circle, above the level of the pier arches, by squinches, two of which are still visible, the remainder having been cunningly concealed by the 18th-century decoration. The dome itself is composed of interlocking amphorae as in the Mausoleum of Galla Placidia, and the whole of the central area is surrounded by an ambulatory supporting a gallery broken on the east by the presbytery. The cross-

34

vaults connecting with the outside walls are later in date than the rest. The entrance and narthex are not where one would expect them to be, opposite the apse, but tacked asymmetrically on to one of the side walls; an arrangement so extraordinary as to suggest that for some reason or other, probably a change in the water-table, the original narthex had to be replaced by another on entirely new foundations.

The most spectacular, if not necessarily the finest, of the celebrated mosaics are undoubtedly the two great panels flanking the apse showing Justinian and Theodora in all their glory. Although hieratically posed, full-face in conventional attitudes, we are left in no doubt that these are real people, not only the two principals but also their attendants, and perhaps the most astonishing thing about these portraits is the incredibly skilful way in which the artist has successfully combined extreme realism in the treatment of the heads, achieved through an advanced illusionist technique (notice particularly the minute spots of brilliant scarlet on the face of the Archbishop and the deep crimson tesserae outlining Theodora's eyelids), with the flat decorative handling of the robes.

Impressive as these two panels most certainly are, the brilliance and elaboration of the frames by which they are surrounded may possibly seem a little too much of a good thing, and it may well be with some slight sense of relief that the visitor turns to the more restrained colour and more sober grandeur of the mosaics in the apse. Here a youthful Christ of extraordinary majesty is seated in glory between two archangels and attended by S. Vitale, in full Byzantine court-dress, and Archbishop Ecclesius, bearing a model of the church. Above His head the sky is streaked with those conventional, multi-coloured clouds which also appear in the apse of S. Costanza in Rome and in S. Apollinare in Classe. Every inch of the surrounding area is covered with the most elaborate and beautiful decoration, all in some way symbolic of the Eucharistic Sacrifice. Floating angels bear aloft circular plaques charged with the Sacred Monogram; birds symbolising incorruptibility drink from the fountain of life; at the summit of the vault the Lamb of God is adored by angels. On one's left, looking eastward, is a lunette in which Abraham entertains the Three Angels (representing the Trinity) on one side and on the other is stopped from sacrificing Isaac by the hand of God emerging from a cloud. Above are Moses on Sinai and Jeremiah contemplating a scroll, below are the evangelists with their symbols, and opposite, Abel and Melchizedek contemplate a table spread in the sight of the Lord; all set in that strange landscape of lurching, flat-topped rocks which was still doing duty for the wilderness in 15th-century Siena.

The sumptuousness of the mosaics is here fully matched by the quality of the three-dimensional decoration. Capitals, impost-blocks and string courses are all superbly carved and drilled and are undoubtedly the product of the great Imperial stonemasons' yards on the Proconnesus. Equally splendid are the pillars and the marble revetment of the lower walls, all properly polished and gleaming, as those in Hagia Sophia so conspicuously are not.

S. Apollinare in Classe. Formerly the magnificent Romanesque campanile dominated a flat, empty landscape, like the tower of some great Fenland church, compelling and remote; today the lorries churn by on the autostrada fringed with gas-stations and pull-ins, while from the direction of Ravenna the apartment blocks and housing estates draw annually nearer. But even now the exterior retains an air of age-old, imperturbable aloofness, and the moment one enters one is in a totally different world.

This is unquestionably the most beautiful of all basilicas—perhaps the most beautiful of all places of Christian worship. Lacking any hint of Gothic mystery, untouched by the intellectualism of the Renaissance or the emotion of the Baroque, it relies entirely for its effect on the beauty of its proportions; all is simple, spacious and drenched in light. By comparison Torcello seems too high, S. Apollinare Nuovo too narrow, while its closest rival, S. Sabina in Rome, has been ruined by those ghastly modernistic paintings round the chancel arch.

The admirably spaced arcades of the aisles are supported on pillars of beautifully veined grey marble with capitals which might well be described as 'gale-torn' acanthus, so flattened are the leaves. (Similar capitals are worked into the Gothic arcade below the palace of the Municipio in Ravenna's principal square, probably taken from the original duomo many times rebuilt.) Above them are no processions of martyrs but simply saints' heads in roundels, faded and inoffensive, dating from the 16th century, but to make up for their absence the mosaics in the apse are more than adequate compensation. In the middle zone S. Apollinare, the first bishop of Classe and a friend of St. Peter, stands with hands outstretched in the formal attitude of prayer, with, in the sky above streaked with the familiar, cigar-shaped clouds, a great star-spangled disk bearing a cross, flanked by Moses and Elias and by three sheep, two on one side and one on the other, the whole scene being presumably a symbolic representation of the Transfiguration. The

S. Fosca, Torcello

exquisite green meadow in which he stands is dotted with Noah's Ark trees in the branches of which are perched innumerable delightful little birds.

Beneath his feet twelve sheep stand in for the apostles and advance towards the centre from right and left. On the chancel arch are more sheep and a medallion of Christ. In the lower zone, in panels between the windows, are classically draped saints standing beneath golden canopies, and, to right and left, are a pair of court groups, similar to those in S. Vitale but far, far inferior in workmanship. However, these last are the only mosaics which are inferior; elsewhere all the borders and acanthus scrolls seem to me just as fine, as regards technique, as those in S. Vitale, but subtler in colour and more restrained in design. Notice particularly the formalised, almost John Piper, columns in the window returns.

In the side aisles are ranged a collection of superb sarcophagi, mainly dating from the 5th and 6th centuries, of the greatest beauty and interest. On going out do not miss a tablet on the south wall of the narthex erected by the grateful people of Ravenna to the memory of that extraordinary figure 'Popski' (Vladimir Peniakoff), whose private army liberated the city in 1945; and, having read, do not fail to say a prayer for the repose of his soul, as it is largely due to his presence of mind and forbearance that the beauty which you have just seen survives intact today.

TORCELLO

The Cathedral. As early as the 7th century the island of Torcello was already the most prosperous in the lagoon, but from the rise of Venice in the 9th its importance steadily declined and it finally lapsed into that state of melancholy abandonment which inspired one of Ruskin's most moving passages. Today all that remains of its former grandeur are the cathedral and the church of S. Fosca.

The cathedral was founded in the 7th century, completely rebuilt in the 9th, and much altered, and heightened, in the 11th. The aisle arcades, which rest on pillars of Greek marble with a surface like watered silk, together with the very beautiful mosaic floor, date from the last rebuilding; at the same time the elaborate ambo, or pulpit, was enlarged and not very skilfully refashioned from the sculptured slabs of some earlier structure which Ruskin believed to have been brought from the mainland. In fact it seems more likely that they were imported from Constantinople, as the exquisite shafts and panels of the iconostasis most certainly were. Do not fail to notice the northernmost panel of two peacocks drinking from a raised chalice, which is rightly judged to be one of the great masterpieces of Byzantine sculpture; the subject, a favourite in the Eastern Church, symbolises the flesh made incorruptible through the Eucharist, but the motif, of two confronted birds or animals on either side of a pillar, long predates Christianity in the Mediterranean world, going back to Mycenean times.

The large apse is dominated by the wonderful figure of the Virgin and Child, unattended by angels, isolated and alone in the vast golden emptiness of the dome. This is a work of the 12th century and may possibly have replaced an earlier representation of the Pantokrator. Below are the twelve apostles ranged round the half-circle of the apse. In order to counteract the optical illusion caused by the curved ground, the two outermost figures, it is claimed, are wider and more thickset than their fellows. Close personal investigation (short, admittedly, of measuring) has convinced me that today this is only true of the apostle on the south, which suggests that his opposite number was at some time or other restored by a mosaicist on whom this 11th-century subtlety was lost. Below the apostles, the bishop's throne and the half-circle of seats for the attendant clergy remain intact. On the west wall is an enormous and splendid composite mosaic in three zones embracing Christ in Glory, the Crucifixion and the Last Judgement, which is also a work of the middle Byzantine period. As usual the torments of the damned, who include a high proportion of Establishment figures—Emperors, Empresses and Patriarchs, as well as Turks, Huns, and Mahomet himself—are depicted with a very vigorous enthusiasm. Curiously enough the inscription is in Greek whereas those in the apse mosaic, which is certainly the work of Greek craftsmen, are in Latin. The two little flanking apses, together with the mosaics in that on the north, date from the 9th century, as does the pavement of which traces were recently discovered several feet below the existing floor-level.

The exceptionally high campanile which dominates the lagoon—'a rude brick campanile of the commonest Lombardic type', as Ruskin rather haughtily describes it—is of the 12th century. The leaden roof of the basilica itself dates from the 20th, and very ugly it is, wrecking the colour and texture of the whole ensemble.

S. Fosca. The church of S. Fosca is not, as Ruskin thought, far more ancient than the cathedral but considerably later, most of it dating from no earlier than the 12th century. The octagonal plan is of a type which became very popular, particularly in Greece, during the middle Byzantine period but which here appears to have proved a little too sophisticated for the local talent. The octagon is successfully reduced to a (very approximate) circle by squinches on which there rests a drum but no dome, the ceiling being a tent-like construction of wooden rafters. Whether funds ran out, which seems

for various reasons unlikely, or a Greek (or Greek trained) foreman died or went home before completion, or whether the native craftsmen's nerve failed them at the last moment, we shall never know. An alternative theory, for which no evidence as far as I can see today exists, is that there was once a dome which later collapsed. Apart from this one structural compromise the quality of the workmanship, particularly of the pillars and capitals, is high.

Externally the church is surrounded on five sides by an ambulatory with an arcade of very stilted arches resting on very slender shafts, some of which are separated at ground-level by marble slabs, waist high, once elaborately carved but now much weathered. Before a 19th-century restoration carried out under the Austrians, the arms of the cross were lit by large semi-circular windows, now bricked up on the north and south and on the west replaced by three lancets.

The most beautiful feature of the whole church, the exterior of the east end, is one that, owing to its closeness to adjacent buildings, can easily be missed. The main apse, polygonal in plan, is enriched with elaborate bands of decorative brickwork, blind arcading and marble string-courses, a technique common enough at this period in Salonica and the Peloponnese but of which this remains the unique example in the West.

VENICE

S. Marco. At the first wonderful sight of this breath-taking façade there is little enough to recall Byzantium. The Gothic pinnacles, the abundance of three-dimensional statuary, 'the marble foam . . . the wreaths of sculptured spray', the mosaics in the lunettes, the horses of Lysippus, even the extraordinary leaden cupolas above the domes, are all quite alien to the Orthodox tradition. Nevertheless the great building they mask is undoubtedly the work of a Greek architect directly inspired by the Church of the Holy Apostles in Constantinople.

When, in the 9th century, Venice was rapidly acquiring status, the Doge, whose private chapel this was, felt the need for some really impressive relics. This was answered by two merchants of Torcello who nicked the miraculously preserved body of St. Mark the Evangelist from the Patriarch of Alexandria and fiddled it through the Mussulman customs by covering it with the forbidden pork. To accommodate this treasure the first S. Marco, probably also cruciform in plan, as befitted a martyrium, was built early in the 9th century and burnt down and rebuilt at the end of the 10th. This edition, proving inadequate or insufficiently sumptuous, was pulled down and replaced by the present building between 1063 and 1094. Today it is the only remaining intact example of what is sometimes called 'the cross-domed basilica'. (The Holy Apostles at Constantinople vanished long since to make way for the Mosque of the Conqueror and the basilica of S. John at Ephesus is in ruins.) In this plan, which had been evolved half a millennium before the building of S. Marco, not only the central crossing but all four arms are covered with domes.

Although Venice had by now long since rejected the nominal suzerainty of the Eastern Emperor, relations, political, commercial and cultural, remained close, and the employment of Greek craftsmen was not only natural but provided abundant and conspicuous proof of the wealth at the Republic's command. But as the years went on, and work continued on the fabric for centuries, Romanesque influences from the nearby mainland began to assert themselves. The most interesting evidence of the resultant stylistic miscegenation is, perhaps, that provided by the five great portals. These concentric arches of elaborately carved stone are clearly Romanesque in inspiration but are supported, not, as elsewhere in the West, by grouped statues but by clustered Byzantine pillars. The narthex, into which they lead, is remarkable for being extended all round the western arm of the cross and including a baptistry on the south side.

The first impression afforded by the interior is one of mysterious, gold-shot gloom, an effect that is frequently regarded as particularly Byzantine. This, of course, is nonsense; the Greeks at all periods have always demanded an abundance of light and the average Orthodox church, particularly on the upper levels, is, by comparisons with Romanesque or Gothic cathedrals, flooded in it. To this rule S. Marco was no exception, but during the course of time most of the original windows were blocked up by Venetian artists avid for more flat areas to cover with decoration. To the resulting darkness a peculiar feature of the lay-out is in part due—the extraordinary cat-walks separating the nave and aisles. Originally the nave arcades supported wide galleries extending to the lateral walls, but so dangerously dark did the shadow they cast eventually become that they had to be removed. An additional reason may possibly have been that there they were unnecessary; the Western rite to which Venice adhered did not so limit the space available to the congregation during services as to justify the vast galleries of Hagia Sophia or S. Irene. Another unusual feature, although one quite without liturgical significance, is the division of the four great piers supporting the central dome by small intersecting barrel vaults on two levels; a device which brilliantly counteracts the feeling of oppressiveness which otherwise their mass might well induce.

The chronology of the mosaics which seem to cover every available inch of the structure internally is complicated and disputable. The earliest (12th century) are those on either side of the main entrance from the narthex into the body of the church; almost contemporary with them are those in the dome above the nave and some of those in the north transept. In the narthex are Old Testament scenes dating from the 13th century and most probably based on a very early Byzantine manuscript of which a copy is in the British Museum. They are distinguished by two qualities rather commoner in Romanesque than Byzantine art—charm and a strong narrative sense, both of which are clearly in evidence in the scene where the children of Israel are gathering manna in the wilderness. These mosaics, given their date, are strangely *avant-garde*, and foreshadow, particularly in their handling of space and their use of architecture, the mature Palaeologan style of the mosaics in the narthex of the Kahriye Djami, almost certainly completed at least half a century later. Oddly enough the most traditionally Byzantine of all the scenes in S. Marco are those in the Baptistry which date from a period, the 14th century, when, even here, Romanesque was already giving way to Gothic. (Note particularly the angels' heads in the Baptism scene.)

Up to the end of the 12th century the decoration of this great church was largely the result of peaceful East–West collaboration, but after the lamentable sack of Constantinople in 1204, of which the Venetians were the principal beneficiaries, the examples of Byzantine craftsmanship which today enliven the fabric were almost all the spoils of war. Apart from many of the enrichments and additions to the celebrated Pala d'Oro (itself, however, commissioned and paid for many years before), these trophies take the form of sculptured marble slabs, of all periods but of the highest quality, covering the whole range of Byzantine decorative art. Confronted birds, winged griffons, lions devouring deer, knot work and entrelacs, all are here. The most familiar and easily appreciable are those on the south wall facing the Piazetta, but those on the north, although less conspicuous, are no whit inferior either in beauty or interest.

3

ALONG THE VIA EGNATIA

WITH the removal of the Imperial Capital from Rome to Constantinople, the Via Egnatia became the most important thoroughfare in the Empire. Starting on the Adriatic coast at Dyrrachium (Durazzo) it crossed the mountains in the neighbourhood of Lake Ochrid, descended into the Macedonian Plain north of Kastoria and ran straight to Thessaloniki, whence it continued across Thrace via Adrianople to the Great City itself. While trade and travellers with time to spare continued to pass between the two parts of the Empire by sea, couriers, envoys, armies and all those in a hurry kept to the road. Of the cities along the route the most important was Thessaloniki; from here subsidiary roads branched out to the Balkans via the Vardar Gap, to Thessaly and Southern Greece by passes over the Pindus. It was not surprising, therefore, that, particularly in later times, the style of building evolved in this great communications centre should have proved the dominant influence in the architectural development of the whole Balkan area.

Today the road's course is marked by the presence of some of the most splendid and important masterpieces still remaining from the Byzantine world. In the north-west are the Serbian churches in the neighbourhood of Lake Ochrid which, with their high drums and elaborate brickwork, would seem to proclaim an obvious indebtedness to Thessalonian example; at Kastoria are innumerable churches and chapels, small in size but highly individual in style; to the north in Bulgaria are still to be found buildings in which the influence of Middle Byzantine developments in Greece is combined with an earlier native tradition dating back to the time of the first Bulgarian Empire; Thessaloniki can today boast more and better churches than Constantinople itself, Hagia Sophia alone excepted; while a day's sail to the south lies the celebrated promontory of Mount Athos.

Kastoria

Occupying a small isthmus connecting the shore with a rocky headland jutting out into the Lake, and surrounded on all sides except the south-east by mountains, Kastoria has as charming a situation as any town in Greece. In late Roman times it rejoiced, according to some authorities, in the resounding name of Diocletianopolis, but later lost this distinction when it passed into the hands of the Bulgarians who retained it until their defeat, by the Emperor Basil the Second, which established Byzantine sway over most of what is today Serbia and Bulgaria, as well as northern Greece. Subsequently it passed back and forth between Greeks, Bulgarians and Franks, and was even held for a short time in the 11th century by an Anglo-Saxon contingent serving in the Byzantine army, including, doubtless, veterans of Hastings, who were finally overwhelmed by their old enemies coming down from Dyrrachium under the command of Robert Guiscard. In the later Empire it achieved a great commercial importance which it retained under the Turks, remaining until well into the 19th century the centre of the fur trade for south-eastern Europe, and which is today reflected in the small size and large number of its churches. For these were not, as elsewhere in Byzantine lands, imperial or ecclesiastical foundations, but owe their origin to the family pride of the local merchants, many of whom are commemorated in the numerous 'donor-portraits'. The period of Bulgarian rule has left its mark in the church-plans, the overwhelming majority of which conform to the simple oblong hall as developed in Bulgaria itself. The elaborate external decoration in brick, albeit rather less sophisticated than in southern Greece, is typically Middle Byzantine in character and suggests that most of these churches were built in the 11th century, presumably before 1080 when the town fell to the Normans.

The Anagyroi. This certainly is the most sophisticated and possibly the oldest church in the town, said by some to have been founded in the 10th century

The Anagyroi, Kastoria

by the Bulgarian Tsar Samuel, but undoubtedly almost completely rebuilt in the 11th after the liberation. It is basilical in plan, with a very high barrel-vaulted *naos* towering above the aisles which show signs of having been at one time also barrel-vaulted, now heavily buttressed on the north. The brickwork decoration in the pseudo-Cufic manner is of the highest quality, the small two-light windows are beautifully recessed and the marble mouldings round the doors most delicately carved. The wall-paintings, which include a recently uncovered Christ between the Virgin and St. John, are attributed to the 11th century, but are difficult to see. In the south aisle are a splendid pair of donor-portraits, the wife very dressy in an enormous turban and scarlet robes, with long blonde curly hair falling over her shoulders.

The Panaghia Koubedeliki. A central dome resting on a very high drum marks this as being the only church in the town which does not conform to the basilical plan. It is a simple triconch, that is to say the projecting transepts

and apse are all three semi-circular, to which has been added a very wide narthex with the west wall painted externally. The brickwork decoration is very spirited, if rather less refined than that of the Anagyroi. Inside are extensive wall-paintings in which it seems that two different artists have had

45

a hand; one, presumably the earlier, being responsible for a very beautiful, almost Hellenistic, head of an angel, but most of whose handiwork has been heavily repainted; the other, altogether more naïf, represented by the well-preserved and charming Nativity on the inside of the west wall in which, although it conforms closely to the accepted canon, a very dashing use of colour suggests a highly individual personality at work. There may well be more accomplished renderings of this familiar scene in Byzantine art, but few so wholly enjoyable. On the outside is a charming Salome doing a scarf dance while balancing the charger with the Baptist's head on her own.

S. Stephanos. Here the customary basilical plan has undergone some curious structural modifications. The *naos* is covered with an exceptionally high barrel vault and separated from the narthex by another set transversely,

which, although lower, completely dominates the aisles. In the north-west corner of the narthex is a staircase going up to the galleries. The paintings are in poor condition and difficult to see. The exquisite carved iconostasis to which the *Guide Bleu* carefully draws the visitor's attention does not, in fact, exist.

The Chapel of the Taxiarchs. Standing close to the dismal modern metropolis is a small hall-church containing, as the dedication would lead one to expect, a great many portraits of military saints. The remainder of the paintings, which include the Dormition and the customary canonical series, are

46

Macedonian in style dating from the 14th century, and relate to similar cycles in the Serbian churches.

S. Nicholaos Kasnitzki. The paintings in this church are the best examples of the Macedonian school to be found in Kastoria. They are conceived on a very grand scale; the figures of the Panaghia and two angels in the apse are almost life-size and disposed in a very masterly way, while the heads of the mourning apostles in the Dormition are exceptionally moving and intense. In the narthex is a pair of donor-portraits.

The Prodromos. This small church, which appears on the map under a purely arbitrary dedication to Hagios Panteleimon, is clearly the 'chicest' church in town. The sanctuary is very dolled up with a lot of hideous modern icons, an abundance of artificial flowers and some plastic lamps of a quite singular horror. The paintings are confined to the east wall and the apse but include a near-masterpiece, the Ascension. This astonishing work is tremendously agitated and convulsive, with the Panaghia the only static figure amidst a crowd of apostles registering astonishment with every variety of gesture and attitude. Although technically less accomplished, it seems to have been touched by a gust of the same wind that blows through the great Anastasis in the Kahriye Djami in Constantinople.

S. Nicholaos. Another hall-church, standing almost opposite the Prodromos, of which the interior is completely covered with a peculiarly grisly set of martyrdoms. Presumably 14th century in date, they are of a purely specialised interest.

S. Pavlos Petros (?). Very close to the principal hotel is a small chapel un-mentioned in any guide-book, the dedication of which I was never able to discover, but which a process of elimination suggests might be a church marked under this name on the map. It is worth searching out for the sake of a singularly fine donor-portrait of a young man in a high fez, at least twice the size of the adjacent saints, that is almost Chinese in its delicacy and feeling.

S. Thomas and The Two Theodores. By rights neither of these two churches deserves mention in a work dealing with Byzantine art, but they are both so charming in their own way that only the most besotted purist would wish to pass them by unvisited. The former is very wide with arcades of well-spaced, high, thin pillars topped with elaborately gilded capitals, separating nave and aisles. At the west end is a delicately curved gallery charmingly decorated with Turkish rococo curlicues, and the ceiling has painted panels divided by pine-wood mouldings and strap-work.

The latter is similar in style but not quite so sumptuous. The gallery is plain, but the ceiling has three very shallow saucer domes painted with flowers and landscapes in a manner similar to that employed in the decoration of the few remaining 18th-century merchants' houses in the lower town. Both churches are very close in style to those in Plovdiv which represent the high water mark of what is described locally, with considerable pride, as 'Bulgarian Renaissance', a style which in fact flourished throughout the Ottoman Empire during the 18th and 19th centuries and is as well represented in the yalehs on the Bosphorus as it is in Bulgaria, and of which the last traces are today to be found on gypsies' carts and canal barges.

The Monastery of the Mavrovitissa. The larger of the two churches in this charmingly situated lakeside monastery, about half an hour's walk from the centre of the town, is painted with an almost complete set of Our Lord's miracles in a good state of preservation. The monastic buildings, shaded by gigantic planes, are indistinguishable architecturally from domestic work of the same date.

Kalabaka and the Meteora

From Kastoria the road runs south-east via Grevena, across uplands covered with dwarf oaks to the foothills of the Pindus. Here is the town of Kalabaka with, immediately behind it, an extraordinary geological formation of grouped limestone pillars and pinnacles, some of considerable height, almost all with vertical sides, on the tops of which are perched a number of monasteries, most of them in ruins.

The cathedral of Kalabaka is marked architecturally by an extreme conservatism. If, as is usually stated, it was built in the early 14th century by the Emperor Andronicus Palaeologos, it must be the very last basilica to be erected in the Byzantine world; it almost certainly occupies the site of a much earlier building which one can only assume enjoyed so great a reputation as to dictate the layout of its successor, built at a date when the cross-in-square plan was everywhere else triumphant. The interior is of the highest interest not only for its archaic plan but also for the number of the original fittings that have survived. The *naos*, which is screened from the aisles by an arcade of alternate pillars and piers, is divided from the sanctuary by a beautiful marble iconostasis, the apse retains a three-tiered *synthronon* half-circling a marble, cone-topped *baldacchino* over the Holy Table, and there is an intact marble ambo supported on six marble columns, plus one of *verde antico* and one of porphyry. There are also fragments of the original paving and paintings on the walls of the aisles, but these latter are of no great distinction. During the last war most of the town was burnt down by the Italians and when I first visited it the church was in a fearful state; today it

has been put back into good shape without, mercifully, over-restoration. Visitors should be warned that it is (or was) haunted by an elderly n'er-do-well masquerading as a verger who stinks to high heaven and possesses an inexhaustible fund of misinformation.

The celebrated monasteries of the Meteora owe their fame to their extraordinary situation rather than to any great architectural distinction. Today, when the impression of inaccessibility has been much modified by the construction of a motor-road, they are best viewed from below. Originally founded as hermitages in the troubled years of the 14th century, they at one time numbered twenty-four, but were reduced to seven by the beginning of the present century, of which today only three are reasonably intact. The largest and highest (148 ft. vertical ascent) is the *Meteoron* founded in 1388 but many times rebuilt. Architecturally quite satisfying in a conventional way, the church is covered with paintings, including a portrait of the founder, which have been recently and all too lovingly restored. One's general impression is of a superabundance of golden haloes, intolerably bright.

The Varlaam, not quite so lofty but formerly even less accessible, possesses two churches, the larger of which was built in the 16th century and restored in the 18th. Neither the architecture nor the paintings are of any particular merit.

S. Stephanos is even less interesting and has the disadvantage of being a nunnery. Greek nuns are almost invariably bossy and frequently off their heads; these, who are no exception, have long since abandoned contemplation for the promotion of sales of the hideous local embroidery. All three churches can boast, and do, the possession of carved, wooden iconostases of a fiendish ingenuity better employed in the decoration of cuckoo clocks.

THESSALONIKI

As the home of one of the first Christian communities on the European mainland, twice visited by the Apostle Paul, the city, already a flourishing commercial centre, acquired after the Peace of the Church a new and distinguished status. With the transference of the capital to Byzantium, with which it enjoyed rapid and easy communications both by sea and land, its position was still further exalted, and when in the 9th century Antioch and Alexandria both fell to the Arabs it became the second most important city in the Eastern Empire. Even more than that of most cities of comparable antiquity its history has been marked by appalling outbreaks of carnage and violence, from that fearful day in A.D. 392 when the homosexual misdemeanours of a popular charioteer provoked a riot which so infuriated the Emperor Theodosius that he massacred over fifteen thousand of the inhabitants in a single afternoon, to the even more terrible months in 1943/4 when the Germans transported a far larger number of the ancient Sephardic Jewish community to the gas-ovens. In the interval it had been occupied by Goths, Avars, Arabs, Normans, Bulgars, Venetians and Turks, and each change of ownership had invariably been followed by large-scale slaughter, and in 1912 it was bombarded by sea and land by the liberating Greeks. In addition to the vindictiveness of man it also suffered a succession of appalling conflagrations which regularly wiped out whole quarters of the town and of which the last, and worst, broke out in 1917 during the Anglo-French occupation.

It is, therefore, little short of miraculous that Thessaloniki has managed to retain so many buildings of historic and aesthetic value relatively intact; long stretches of walls, less extensive but better preserved than those of Constantinople, still encircle it on the landward side and of its many churches seven at least are of the first importance.

S. Georgios. Under the later Roman Empire there stood, a little to the south of the present Via Egnatia and on a line with the still existing Arch of Galerius, an extensive Imperial Palace to which was attached an enormous circular building, perhaps an audience-hall, perhaps the mausoleum of the Emperor Galerius himself. At some time around A.D. 400 this was converted into a church by the addition of an apse, an entrance porch and an encircling ambulatory, and such it remained until its perversion into a mosque in the 16th century when the ambulatory was removed. After the liberation of 1912 it reverted to being a place of Christian worship but subsequently lapsed into museum status. The original construction was simple and remains relatively intact; in a circular brick wall of remarkable thickness are eight niches, of which that on the east was incorporated in the apse on the building's conversion into a church, when the remainder were opened out into the ambulatory. It was lit by eight round-headed windows (two now bricked up) and eight lunettes immediately below the drumless dome which today is covered by a timber roof but which may formerly have been visible externally, as in the Pantheon. Most of the mosaic decoration with which the interior was covered at the time of its conversion has long since vanished, but what remains is quite sufficiently astonishing.

In the lower zone of the dome are a series of panels of a grandeur and originality without parallel in early Christian, or indeed Byzantine, art. Against a glittering, golden cyclorama, visible through the numerous openings, is set an extraordinary display of fantastic architectural perspectives—columns and cornices, niches and arcades, fluted half domes and conches, draped with curtains and enlivened with peacocks—in front of which there stand at regular intervals saints and martyrs, nearly life-size but almost overwhelmed by the scale and grandeur behind them. Rather naturalistically conceived, with elaborately draped robes and hands extended in the 'orans' position, these are singularly fine examples of a type that constantly recurs throughout the Byzantine world; but the architectural setting is unique. Very small-scale and comparatively unsophisticated perspective niches appear, it is true, behind the Hetoimisia in the dome of the Orthodox Baptistry in Ravenna, and the pages of certain manuscripts, notably the S. Medard Codex in the Bibliothèque Nationale are somewhat similarly decorated, but nothing on this elaborate scale exists elsewhere. Open arcaded perspectives were already a popular form of wall-decoration in Roman times, of which numerous examples are to be found at Pompeii, and may well have provided at second or third hand the original inspiration, but it has been suggested, in my view rightly, that these structurally perfectly consistent fantasies derive directly from the stage settings known to have been employed in the great theatre at Antioch. Indeed, I would go further and, speaking for once from personal experience, put forward the view that they are, in fact, the work of a professional stage designer carried out in mosaic, so sure is the control of perspective and so firm the grasp of the third dimension.

In the zone immediately above were formerly a row of standing apostles, traces of whose feet are still faintly discernible, and in the dome itself was a full-length Pantokrator in a *mandorla* supported by four angels. On the north wall of the apse is an indifferently preserved painting of St. Andrew.

The only other remaining mosaics are to be found on the vaults of the surrounding niches, which are patterned with flowers, birds and miscellaneous débris in a smart interior decorator's style, known as 'asaroton' (i.e. unswept), first introduced by Sosos of Pergamon and very popular under the late Empire, which also occurs in S. Costanza in Rome, but which, while well suited to the decoration of pavements, produces a rather less happy effect when applied to walls and ceilings.

The Paraskevi. Sometimes referred to by pedants as the church of the Acheiropoetos, a name which it bore before the Turkish conquest, this church, although frequently restored, perfectly represents the second stage in the development of the basilica and dates from the mid-5th century. An oblong hall of three aisles, the outermost supporting galleries, with an apse and narthex, it once possessed both an exo-narthex and an *atrium* of which the former was still standing as late as the end of the last century. The columns separating the nave and aisles are monolithic, with Corinthian capitals on the ground floor and Ionic capitals with impost-blocks at gallery level. The soffits of some of these arcades still retain their original mosaic decoration— rather charming formalised baskets of fruit and flowers, very bright in colour

and strangely reminiscent of the Lovat Fraser designs which used to illumin-
ate the broadsheets of the Poetry Bookshop. The fragments of frescoes on the
outer wall are modern.

S. Demetrios. If the Paraskevi can be classified as the perfect example of the
second stage of the development of the basilica, S. Demetrios represents the
culmination. Founded, possibly, at the end of the 5th century, it was partially
rebuilt after a fire in the 7th along the original lines; from time to time undergoing various restorations, occasioned by more fires or enemy action, it
remained virtually intact until the 20th century when it was gutted, but
mercifully not destroyed, by the great fire of 1917. Roofless and calcined,
it still remained enormously impressive until the late 'forties when it was
completely restored. Today it stands, soulless and pretentious, a fearful
example of exactly how restoration should not be carried out.

Mercifully, while the original decoration of the interior has largely been
replaced by whitewash or ill-conceived refacing in the cheapest possible
marble, the noble proportions remain unmodified. An enormous nave,
40 ft. × 108 ft., is flanked by four aisles, supporting galleries and surmounted by a clerestory, separated from the nave by arcades made up of
two piers and ten columns, of white marble, porphyry and *verde antico*,
topped by the finest examples of 'wind-blown' acanthus capitals existing in
the world today, not excepting Ravenna. The aisles themselves are divided
by rows of eleven columns originally in *verde antico*. In addition, at the east
end immediately in front of the apse, as in old S. Peter's, there project two
short, aisled transepts of which the southern covers a small crypt, now a
museum. To the south near the spot where the staircase goes down to the
crypt have been discovered the foundations of a small church with an apse
that was almost certainly the original shrine over which the first basilica
was built. Attached to the eastern wall of the southern transept which, like
its partner, projects externally beyond the curve of the apse, is the small
three-aisled chapel of S. Euthymios, decorated with 14th-century paintings
of the Macedonian school, closely relating to contemporary work in the
Lake Ochrid area, covering an earlier series. The tomb of the saint, which
was formerly one of the most important pilgrimage shrines of the Byzantine
world, is either in a small chapel off the north-west end of the nave, or, as
some maintain, in the crypt. In the south aisle is a very spirited battle-piece
showing barbarians sacking a church, presumably the 5th-century foundation, with the female members of the congregation, clearly anticipating a fate

53

worse than death, in the flame-wreathed gynaeceum, and a dashing rescue party led by a mounted Emperor advancing rapidly from the left.

However, it is not to its wall-paintings but to its few remaining mosaics that S. Demetrios today owes its fame. In Byzantium the tradition of portraiture inherited from Hellenistic Egypt flourished continuously throughout a period when it had almost completely vanished in the West, not to re-emerge until Gothic times. Apart from the Imperial likeness, which every shop and place of business was forced by law to display, and those of bishops and high-ranking officials which adorned so many of the churches, portable portraits, usually in encaustic, of ordinary citizens existed in large numbers although none have survived. (In the capital itself there was even a wholesale production of 'pin-ups', pictures of the most popular courtesans and dancers of the day which enjoyed a wide circulation and commanded high prices.) Of this art the finest examples that exist today are the series, some of which were only discovered after the fire, attached to the piers in the nave, probably at various times during the 7th century. Thoughtful and grave, but not severe, strictly frontal in their pose, these saints, bishops and donors seem to possess an intense inner life of their own as they gaze down detached, but not wholly indifferent, on the worshipper and the tourist. Their faces are less naturalistic in the rendering than those in the great Imperial scenes at S. Vitale, their robes are even more formalised and the colour is far more restrained. That they are in many cases true portraits and not imaginary concepts or artists' models is indicated by the fact that some of them are provided with the square halo of the living. Everyone will have his own favourite among these masterpieces, but to my mind the two finest are a donor with his two children, and Demetrios between a bishop and the prefect Leontius.

Externally the church is infinitely depressing; scraped and repointed in a loathsome red, it is guaranteed to discourage; only on the east where, anyhow on my last visit, the ancient brickwork is left untouched, can one fully appreciate the noble proportions undistracted by the surface decoration.

Hosios David. Sometimes referred to as the Sanctuary of Christ Latomos, this small church, tucked away close to the walls in the upper town, was formerly attached to a long-vanished monastery. Probably dating from the mid-5th century, it is a domed cruciform with angle-chambers, a plan which the experts carefully distinguish from the later cross-in-square, arguing that here the chambers are, in fact, the supporting piers hollowed out and not new additions, which some might consider a distinction rather than a difference. However, it is not the partially ruined fabric—the dome has gone and only the pendentives remain—but the splendid mosaic in the half-dome over the apse, only discovered shortly after the last war, that fully justifies the steep climb. Representing the vision of Ezekiel, a beardless Christ, right hand upraised, the left holding a scroll, is seated in glory flanked by two prophets and the evangelistic beasts. The whole is Hellenistic in feeling, particularly in the treatment of the fragmented landscape in the background, and the central figure is of an exceptional dignity that recalls that of the Good Shepherd in the Mausoleum of Galla Placidia at Ravenna, with which it is almost contemporary.

Hagia Sophia. About no church in the Byzantine world has there been more dispute between the experts than this. The dates suggested for its erection range between the early 6th century and the 8th; it used to be maintained that it predated its namesake in Constantinople and the claim has even been put forward that this is the first dome successfully to be raised on pendentives, which is manifest nonsense. My own personal theory is that work had just started when the first dome of Hagia Sophia in the capital collapsed (A.D. 558) and the alarmed builders had then seriously to modify their original plans. This at least would explain the clumsy, almost octagonal shape of the drum as being due to a hasty and unforeseen increase in the size of the piers. However, all that can be said with certainty (from the evidence of the mosaics in the apse) is that the church was virtually completed before the outbreak of the Iconoclastic Controversy in A.D. 726.

The plan is a domed cruciform surrounded by very wide aisles opening into the narthex on the west, with three apses externally on the east, of which that in the centre is separated from the *naos* by an additional bay. The supporting piers of the dome are pierced by arches on two levels. It must be freely admitted that the church's unquestioned historical interest is hardly matched by its aesthetic appeal; structurally clumsy, the lamentable painted decoration, dating from the time of its reconversion to a church in 1912, does nothing to conceal the heaviness of the proportions; the capitals of the pillars, in many cases seemingly squashed by the weight of their impost-blocks, cannot be compared with those in S. Demetrios; externally it is only to be distinguished from a Turkish barracks by the presence of a low dome rising above a square base on a squat drum.

Nor, with one exception, are the remaining mosaics of any outstanding quality; in the apse is a slightly megalocephalic Virgin and Child with, behind Her, the outline of the large cross which was the sole decoration permitted by the Iconoclasts. This replaced an earlier Virgin, traces of whose footstool are still faintly discernible. At the summit of the dome is a seated pentecostal Christ supported by angels, rather clumsy and unrefined, but in the zone immediately below is one of the most remarkable compositions in the whole of Byzantine art.

The conception of a ring of apostles, with, in this case, the addition of the Panaghia and two angels, separated by formalised palm trees, surrounding a central figure of Christ is sufficiently familiar, but here we are in a completely different world from that in which the apostles in the dome of the Orthodox Baptistry have their dignified being. These convulsive and schematised figures are the Demoiselles d'Avignon of Byzantine art, as far removed in feeling from their predecessors in Ravenna as are Picasso's maidens from the odalisques of Ingres. One has a strong impression that here something quite new was happening and that henceforth Byzantine artists might well go off on a quite different, possibly cubist, tack, antedating by more than a millennium the work of such neo-Orthodox artists as Larionov and Goncharova. That this development never, in fact, occurred encourages one to believe that this composition is considerably earlier than the central figure in the dome, and than the date usually suggested, for the one thing which could have cut short so promising a movement could only, surely, have been Iconoclasm. In support of this theory I would cite the extravagantly contorted apostle almost opposite the Panaghia—incidentally this must be the only visible backside in the Byzantine world—whose almost dislocated head is shown in profile. For the post-Iconoclastic period the profile was rigorously taboo except in the case of Judas, and it is inconceivable that he should have been included, in an act of adoration such as this, on an equal level with the rest of the apostles.

The Panaghia Chalkeon. The great period of building ushered in by the victories of Basil II has left few traces in Thessaloniki, possibly because the aftereffects of the Arab sack were so severe that all local efforts were directed to the repair and maintenance of the existing buildings; and this, the only church which can safely be assigned to the epoch, is more interesting for the hints it provides of the shape of things to come rather than for its relationship to contemporary work elsewhere in Greece. A cross-in-square with only the crossing and two western angle-chambers covered by domes, it possesses an exo-narthex on two levels. Built entirely of brick, it relies for external effect on a very skilful use of deeply recessed blind arcading, reinforced on the west by semi-circular pilasters also in brick, all designed to provide the vertical emphasis which was to be the hall-mark of Thessalonian architecture in its last phase. It was heavily, but not too badly, restored just before the last war.

The Hagia Ekaterini. The epoch of the Palaeologan Revival, of which this church is perhaps the earliest example, was here particularly glorious architecturally. Here all four corner bays are covered by domes on lofty drums, and both the barrel vaults of the side arms and the apse itself rise high above the roof-line of the encircling narthex. The external decoration takes the form of variegated brickwork recalling that on the chevet of the Fenari Djami in Constantinople; inside, contemporary paintings have been revealed by the removal of layers of Turkish plaster and two of the domes contain mosaics.

The Holy Apostles. This, the most splendid of all the later Byzantine churches, was almost as influential in the development of church architecture in the Balkans and even Russia, as was the Sainte Chapelle in the Gothic West. Here the effect after which the builders both of S. Ekaterini and the Chalkeon were clearly striving is perfectly achieved. It was built early in the 14th century by the contemporary Patriarch of Constantinople. The plan is an elaborate cross-in-square with additional aisles and an exo-narthex, and the overall emphasis is on height, which is stressed not only by raising the drums supporting the five domes, but also by lowering the roof-line of the narthex and outer aisles and by substituting beautifully spaced low arcades, open on the west, for the two rows of windows at Hagia Ekaterini. The east end provides what is perhaps the finest of all examples of the fully developed Byzantine technique of brick decoration; the neo-Cufic devices of the earlier period have here all been absorbed and transformed, and the cloisonné effect formerly attained by the insertion of ceramic-ware and antique fragments has been abandoned in favour of immensely elaborate and perfectly controlled pattern-work obtained by brick-laying alone. Or almost alone, for there are, it is true, here and there contrasting stone insertions, but this polychromatic device, elsewhere carried to rather disquieting lengths, as in Arta, Bulgaria and the Pammakaristos in Constantinople, is here used with the utmost discretion.

The interior is enlivened with some admirable paintings of which the most memorable, if not perhaps the finest, is a very sinuous Salome in the prothesis, dancing with all the carefree assurance of a ballerina assoluta, with the Baptist's head on her own, a theme which we have already seen illustrated in Kastoria. In the dome are mosaics, some of them uncovered since my last visit, which are said to be of high quality.

BULGARIA

At the time of the official establishment of Christianity the inhabitants of Macedonia and Thrace were largely indigenous and the administration was Roman, but as time wore on and barbarian pressure built up beyond the Danube, the racial pattern grew steadily more confused. The first newcomers were the Slavs, driven from their original homeland around the Pripet Marshes by the Avars, who, after centuries of continuous penetration, were finally overwhelmed by a Turanian tribe known to history as the Proto-Bulgars. By the end of the 8th century the latter, who remained a dominant minority in a largely Slav world, had built up an Empire stretching from the Black Sea to the Adriatic. Pagan at first, they were converted to Byzantine Christianity; missionaries from Thessaloniki, SS. Cyril and Methodius provided them with a Slavonic liturgy and the alphabet with which to write it. Having proved an abiding threat to Constantinople for years, their dominion was finally overthrown at the beginning of the 11th century by Basil II who re-incorporated all their Western and Southern provinces into the Empire. Nearly two centuries later, however, Basil's enfeebled successors were unable to prevent the rise of the second Bulgarian Empire, established by the brothers Assen with its capital at Tirnovo, which lasted more or less intact until the coming of the Turks.

All three periods of Bulgarian history have left architectural remains; those of the first are, with the exception of the basilica at Sofia, ruinous or represented solely by their foundations, and those of the second are hardly more numerous or better preserved, but from the third there exist a number of churches and monasteries in which a conservative preference for the simple hall-plan is combined with a fondness for very elaborate polychromatic external decoration and a wide use is made of blind arcading and recessed niches. As Turkish rule was, in Bulgaria, even harsher than in Greece such church-building as went on in Ottoman times was, with very few exceptions, discreet almost to the point of invisibility, and is represented by a handful of minuscule monuments, often partially underground, offering no visual challenge to the adjacent mosques.

S. George. The earliest church in Sofia is that of S. George which, like its namesake in Thessaloniki, represents the conversion of a circular building of pagan origin and uncertain purpose (possibly part of a Roman bath) into a place of Christian worship. Very small, of unadorned brick, it enjoys the unenviable distinction of having the most depressing situation of any church in the Byzantine world; surrounded on all sides by the cliff-like walls of the Hotel Balkan, as monstrous an example of Stalinist neo-classic as can be found on this side of the Dnieper, it makes the setting of the little Metropolis in Athens seem by contrast positively unencumbered.

S. Sophia. Here the singularity of the architecture has given rise to much discussion. At first glance one would be tempted to describe it as a Romanesque basilica, and indeed it has been argued that the plan must have been the result of Western influence, possibly introduced by the Crusaders who several times traversed Bulgaria on their way to the East. Unfortunately for those maintaining such theories, there would seem to be no doubt whatever that the church as it exists today was completed before the Slav invasions in the 7th century, possibly in the middle of the 6th, at a time when of Romanesque, or even for that matter Carolingian, architecture no hint existed. Conceived on a very grand scale, the basilica is built entirely of brick, except for a stone base, and the layout has for a Western visitor a strangely familiar look; a wide vaulted nave with slightly projecting transepts is divided from the aisles by arcades resting on piers, and the crossing is surmounted by a drumless dome, surrounded externally by an octagon, and separated from the semi-circular apse by an additional barrel-vaulted bay. At the west end a narthex runs the whole width of the church surmounted by a gallery. Formerly it was flanked by towers and it seems probable that the aisles also supported galleries. Completely devoid of decoration of any kind, either carved or painted, this great church relies for the undeniably impressive effect that it produces solely on its monumental proportions and the subtlety of its spatial relationships.

The Monastery of Batchkovo. Of the two great Bulgarian monasteries it is Batchkovo which has the more to offer the foreign visitor; its rival, Rila, while arousing far greater enthusiasm among the Bulgarians themselves, for reasons totally unconnected with architecture, was completely gutted and rebuilt in the 19th century, and of the original building only a single not very interesting fortified tower remains.

The Monastery of Batchkovo, on the other hand, is one of the very few buildings in Bulgaria of which the foundation dates from the period of the

Byzantine domination in the 11th century. The founder was a naturalised Armenian of Georgian origin, Grigori Boukiani by name, who amassed a sizeable fortune while Quartermaster General of the Imperial armies, but of whose buildings all that remains today is the funerary chapel he erected for the accommodation of his 'sinful body'. It is on two floors and represents a type of building peculiar to Bulgaria; on ground-level is a vault containing sarcophagi, above is a single-naved church with a semi-circular apse (five-sided externally), a square narthex, and three pairs of pilasters supporting the ribs of a barrel vault. The exterior is elaborately decorated with blind arcading and niches which do not, curiously enough, correspond to the spatial divisions of the internal walls. This method of decoration, which was to become a distinctive feature of Bulgarian church-building, derives, it has been suggested, from Armenia, the adopted homeland of General Boukiani himself.

The little cathedral and the monastic buildings themselves were erected in the 17th century during a period when the Ottoman ban on church-building was provisionally lifted. The layout—a large fortified enceinte surrounded on the inside with arcaded galleries on three levels with free-standing churches and a refectory in the middle—conforms to the usual Athonite pattern, as does the cathedral. This is a cross-in-square, very unusual in Bulgaria, with a dome supported on four pillars over the crossing, the angle-chambers groin-vaulted and with projecting apses attached to the lateral arms of the cross. An unusual feature is the pair of charming little arcaded porches north and south of the narthex which is, itself, covered by a single, concealed dome flanked by barrel vaults.

The situation of the monastery is charming, its condition, in strong contrast to that of so many on Athos, excellent, and the wine, if you can get hold of it, the best in Bulgaria. It still shelters an abbot and a handful of monks who regularly celebrate the Divine Liturgy, while the long rows of empty cells are admirably maintained by the State for the holiday accommodation of ramblers and youth clubs.

Boiana. Of all Bulgarian churches that of Boiana, on the slopes of Mount Vitosha, overlooking Sofia, is the most rewarding. It is, in fact, three tiny chapels joined together longitudinally, of which the earliest, and eastern-most, dates from the 11th century. Square on the outside, the plan has been rendered cruciform internally by building up solid piers in all four corners. The crossing thus achieved is surmounted by a dome supported on a circular drum with wide projecting eaves looped up over the four tiny windows. The north and south walls are enlivened with three niches apiece that fulfil a purely decorative function as they in no way correspond to the internal layout. Of these the central niche, higher than the others, is emphasised by a 'looping-up' of the cornice. To this little chapel a local magnate, the Sebasto-krator Kaloyan, added, in the reign of Constantine Assen (1258–1277), a mortuary chapel similar to that at Batchkovo. Here the ground floor is

occupied by the funerary chamber itself, which is barrel-vaulted and adorned on the north and east walls with arched niches. Above is another small church of which the plan corresponds to that of the older church to the east, but of which the cruciform nature is in this case indicated externally; the drum of the dome is octagonal and the eaves project even further. Formerly, as we can see from the portrait of the Sebastokrator holding his church, the two stories were connected by a wooden staircase externally attached. The third church, that on the west, is nothing but a square 19th-century annex, devoid of all interest.

Fascinating and extraordinary as is the architecture, Boiana's chief claim to fame, and a formidable claim it is, lies in the paintings with which Kaloyan adorned both foundations. These, while conforming more or less to the usual Byzantine iconographical requirements, are infused with a feeling that is, as far as I know, unique. Here, far more strongly than in Mistra, one is haunted by the idea that the Renaissance is at hand. This feeling is, however, purely subjective, as the paintings were completed fifty years before Giotto had started work on the Arena Chapel at a period when Bulgarian contacts with the West were virtually nil. Chiefly remarkable, to me at least, is the representation of Our Lord, which seems to reflect a highly personal relationship between the artist and his subject, quite unparalleled in the Orthodox world. In the scene of the Presentation in the Temple the figure of the Christ child is endowed with an extraordinary vitality quite untinged by sentimentality; the adolescent disputing with the doctors is clearly the same child, a few years older, and with an added gravity; the young man, now bearded, giving his blessing, is the child come to maturity and so vividly conceived as to suggest something in the nature of a direct experience enjoyed by the artist. The Crucifixion, although, perhaps naturally, rather more conventionally presented, is a most moving work in a very beautiful and unexpected range of colours. There are also two pairs of notable portraits, one of the Tsar and Tsarina, the other of the Sebastokrator and his wife in which the figures, despite their conventional trappings, are presented with a naturalism for which one would look in vain in contemporary state-portraiture elsewhere. The artist, it is claimed locally, was a native Bulgarian, a claim which in default of any direct evidence to the contrary it would be reasonable to accept.

Tirnovo, the ancient Capital of the second Bulgarian Empire, remains today one of the most dramatically situated mediaeval towns in Europe, perched on a series of steep bluffs above a sharply winding river. Formerly it was encircled with walls, adorned with Boyars' palaces and dotted with innumerable churches. Of these last only three of any interest remain, all much altered and restored.

S. Demetrius. This small church, very simple in plan with a single nave, an apse and a narthex, dates from the very end of the Byzantine period and was the scene of the declaration of independence by the Assen brothers, which ushered in the Second Empire. The outside walls are decorated with the usual niches and it may once have had a dome over the central area.

The Church of the Forty Martyrs. A basilica with aisles and three apses, a plan common enough during the First Empire but almost unique in the Second, the church was built to commemorate the victory of Ivan Assen II over the Despot of Epirus in 1230, a triumph of which we are grandiloquently re-minded by an inscription on one of the six columns, of which the capitals were taken from some Roman ruins in the neighbourhood. On the west is a curious exo-narthex set at an angle to the main axis and decorated externally with recessed niches enlivened with ceramic plaques. In Ottoman times the church was used as a mosque and has been heavily restored.

SS. Peter and Paul. A cross-in-square, reflecting contemporary trends in Constantinople, this is the most interesting church in the town. The dome is supported on four columns and a further pair separates the central area from the apse; the angle-chambers are barrel-vaulted and a transverse barrel vault covers the narthex which has three entrances. Externally, the octagonal drum supporting the dome is decorated with recessed niches beneath an undulating cornice. Built in the 14th century, this, apart from a couple of ruinous churches on the Black Sea, is the only cross-in-square of this date in the country.

The Monastery of the Preobajensky. The church of this prettily sited and still functioning monastery just outside the town is worth a visit for the sake of its external wall-paintings, late in date but charming. Curiously enough the custom of decorating church exteriors with murals seems to be confined exclusively to the northern areas of the Byzantine world, just where one would have thought climatic conditions were the least favourable. Apart from those in Kastoria the only examples known to me in Greece, outside Athos, are in the neighbourhood of Volo, but in Rumania the practice is, I believe, widespread.

ATHOS

Lavra.

According to tradition this strange and extraordinarily beautiful peninsula was first sanctified by the Virgin Mary herself, who stopped here on her way from Palestine to Cyprus, and at whose advent all the pagan shrines and statues immediately collapsed. From that time forth, while its sanctity remained inviolate, its history was for several hundred years uneventful, or at least, unrecorded. At the very beginning of the 10th century we hear of various hermits living in the remoter fastnesses of the mountain whose relatively simple and uninstructed life was, towards the end of the century, complicated by the arrival of St. Athanasios. This formidable figure was a monk who had for many years enjoyed a position, *vis-à-vis* that tough but neurotic and unamiable general, Nicephorus Phocas, the liberator of Crete, which would in the West have been described as that of Father Confessor. Encouraged by his Imperial charge, who had long entertained the ambition of devoting himself in old age to the contemplative life, Athanasios descended upon Athos and not only started to organise the rather idiosyncratic practice of monasticism that had hitherto flourished, but started to build a monastery into which his distinguished patron could in due course conveniently retire. But then two events occurred which, fortunately only temporarily, disrupted

66

this plan. The middle-aged general fell madly in love with the Empress Theophano who, responding, and her husband conveniently dying, promptly raised Phocas to the purple, an elevation which caused him indefinitely to postpone the fulfilment of his monastic ambitions; and Athanasios, naturally much shaken by this change of plan, returned to Athos where the partially constructed dome of his new foundation fell on him, finally removing his chance of seeing his great work completed, but for ever ensuring his sanctity. However, his enterprise survived him and not only was his own foundation, he Great Lavra, duly completed, but in the following centuries the whole headland was adorned with religious foundations. From then on its history was, by Balkan standards, comparatively tranquil. From time to time pirates descended, occasionally catching a monastery unawares; efforts were made by Iconoclast Emperors to suppress the Holy Pictures, almost always, thanks to the vigilance of the monks and, on many occasions, to the direct intervention of the Panaghia, ineffectual; and the attempts of Latin Emperors to impose the Western rite in due course produced a crop of martyrs, and, it must be admitted, a handful of collaborationists whose indestructible corpses remain in a state of grisly preservation in the Cave of the Wicked Dead. Feuds and disputes between the various monasteries were frequent but only once was the Mountain the scene of a major theological controversy. This arose at the end of the 13th century as the result of the emergence of an Athonite sect known as the Hesychasts who maintained that a prolonged and solitary contemplation of the navel would afford to those with sufficient perseverance a glimpse of the Uncreated Light which had irradiated Mount Tabor at the Transfiguration. This belief, at first condemned as heretical, gained many adherents and was finally accepted by the Orthodox Church in the last years of the Empire, but found, not altogether surprisingly, no expression, as far as I am aware, in art.

Today this long ridge, ending in the most dramatic of all mountains, thrusting down into the Aegean, dotted with monasteries, sanctified by innumerable legends, as unrelentingly masculine as White's Club, remains a fascinating but rapidly crumbling fossil, the abiding inspiration of many of the most highly-charged writers of our time. While the natural beauty of the place abundantly justifies pages of purple prose, the enthusiasm aroused by its architectural features is harder to understand. Enormously picturesque as most of them are, the majority of the existing monasteries approximate, anyhow at first glance, to superb stage settings; the architectural value of the component parts of these extraordinary ensembles is slight, and they seem to belong rather to the world of Bakst and Bibbienna than to that of Palladio or Philibert de l'Orme.

The customary monastic plan is comparatively simple; a circle, or polygon, of formidable walls, reinforced at intervals by watch-towers, supporting on the inside, ranges of buildings varying in style from the most primitive adaptations of the traditional Turkish Khan to the most highly sophisticated examples of Tsarist neo-classic, encloses an open space in which stand a canopied fountain, the *phiale*, the *katholikon* or abbey church, a clock-tower, a varying number of chapels and, occasionally, the refectory. Almost all the larger churches are examples of the multi-domed cross-in-square, first developed in the Middle Byzantine period, modified to suit monastic requirements by the addition of semi-circular apses to the north and south arms of the cross. Frequently they possess not only a narthex and exo-narthex, but also a further external porch known as a *lite*. The drums of the dome are polygonal, usually divided by engaged colonettes flanking doubly recessed windows, topped by leaden roofs with undulating cornices. In several cases, notably those foundations which a closeness to the sea rendered unusually exposed to corsair raids, the area covered was comparatively small and the necessary accommodation could only be achieved by building upwards. The result was a series of skyscraper-like towers topped with three or four courses of projecting balconies, producing a strange, Tibetan effect.

The most immediately striking impression produced by all these buildings is that created by the lavish employment of brilliant colour. Elsewhere in the Byzantine world the brick or stone-work of church exteriors was normally left uncovered, but here it is almost always concealed beneath a coat of paint regularly renewed. The most popular colours are sang-de-bœuf, a rusty pink, Prussian blue and ochre; even when, usually in the smaller churches, the stonework is visible, the tile-courses are heightened with crimson and picked out in white.

All the churches and some of the refectories are covered internally with murals but, as with the architecture, it is the general overall effect which impresses rather than single scenes or portraits. On Athos, where the ancient customs and practices of the Orthodox Church are more stubbornly upheld than elsewhere, the traditional attitude to paintings has always prevailed; cleaning is taboo, and when age, damp and candle-smoke have reduced the legibility of a picture to the point where the subject matter is visible only to the eye of faith, it has firmly been repainted. Thus, while the lines and composition of the original have usually been faithfully adhered to,

68

Vatopedi, Athos

colour and tone values have undergone surprising changes, and in many cases what we see today stands in the same relationship to the original as an 18th-century English copy of a 16th-century Italian Madonna made from a line engraving. If and when some of the finest of the early series, notably those at Vatopedi, have received the expert treatment to which, at the time of my last visit, the icons at the Great Lavra were being subjected, the enthusiasm they aroused in the late Robert Byron and other experts may well be shared by the layman.

Compared, say, with that of Cluny in the West, the architectural and artistic influence of Athos in the Byzantine world was nil. It originated no new forms or plans and during long centuries hardly modified those it had originally inherited from elsewhere; even the layout of the monastic buildings, which was faithfully copied in Bulgaria and elsewhere in the Balkans, had been evolved in Syria and developed in southern Greece centuries before the coming of Athanasios to Chalkidiki. After the fall of the Empire, life continued almost exactly as before; the community's relations with the Turks were always surprisingly good and the suzerainty of the Sultan, who never attempted to interfere in matters of doctrine or internal discipline, may well have come to seem less irksome than that of the Thirteenth Apostle. Isolation from the contemporary world was now complete and in this strange Byzantine enclave in an Islamic Empire there flourished, at a slowly diminishing tempo, a way of life that, save in a few remote spots such as Sinai, had elsewhere become extinct. From time to time there came travellers and bibliophiles from the West who relieved the monks of manuscripts and other treasures the significance of which they had in most cases long since ceased to understand; frescoes were duly renewed and buildings restored and added to in the traditional manner, and, indeed, most of what we see today dates from the twilight years. To describe in detail all the twenty remaining monasteries would, in a work such as this, be tedious and unjustified; I have accordingly selected four which seem to me to be those likely to prove most rewarding for the ordinary visitor, who should, however, be warned that even this reduced round will need time, for not only are mules no longer readily available but at all seasons sudden changes of wind are liable to render the small harbours and anchorages inaccessible. Not only are stout legs and a strong stomach essential but also high spirits, for a powerful melancholy haunts these slopes, and nowhere in the whole Mediterranean does the heart sink so regularly with the sun.

The Protaton. The administrative capital of Athos is the mournful, if picturesque, little village of Caryes. Here are the residence of the civil governor and the assembly-hall of the representatives of the leading monasteries. Opposite the latter stands the church of the Protaton, probably the oldest existing building on the Mountain, so called from the Protos, or first among the brethren to whom the supreme authority was formerly delegated. Alone among the churches of Athos it is a basilica, and its foundation predates the coming of Athanasios who enlarged it, round about A.D. 965, with funds provided by Nicephorus Phocas. At the end of the 13th century it was badly damaged by fire or earthquake but soon restored and decorated with the existing frescoes.

The artist responsible was, according to a long and well-attested tradition, Pansellinos of Thessaloniki, one of the comparatively few Byzantine artists whose identity has survived. However, as the laudatory references to him date largely from the 18th century and, while establishing his personality, fail to mention the exact period at which he flourished, his connection with these particular paintings had formerly to be taken on trust. Recently, however, a careful comparison with contemporary work in Thessaloniki (notably in the Euthymios chapel in S. Demetrios) which all traditions agree was his place of origin, has strengthened the probability of his responsibility. The paintings themselves are among the earliest and finest examples of the Macedonian school, which flourished during the Palaeologan period, chiefly in Northern Greece, Macedonia and Serbia, but of which the influence extended as far south as Mistra. It was characterised by a light palette, a tendency to generalisation, a fondness for large, open forms, and an intensity, particularly in portraiture, almost amounting to expressionism. (The Macedonian artist's approach to his subject matter is sometimes, rather misleadingly, described as realistic, a qualification which can only be justified by comparison with that of the opposing Cretan school.) Here the unusual layout of the frescoes arises from the difficulty of modifying a system evolved for the decoration of the domed cross-in-square to suit a basically basilican plan; they are in four zones, the topmost filled with the ancestors of Christ from Adam onwards, the second with scenes from the life of Christ, the third, which is broken on three sides by arches, by the four Evangelists, and on the unbroken west wall by the Dormition of the Virgin; the lowest and widest is taken up with a whole portrait gallery of saints, hermits and Fathers of the Church. The most interesting and original of these four series is the second, where the various traditional episodes do not occupy self-contained panels, as was the usual practice, but are linked by smaller subsidiary scenes into one continuous narrative band.

While for anyone seriously interested in the development of Byzantine painting a visit to the Protaton is essential, the enthusiast should be warned that the whereabouts of the key is, even by Athonite standards, exceptionally difficult to establish. Indeed, I myself was quite unable to locate it, and the above account is based on what can be seen by energetic clambering up to windows, and on the evidence of the collection of admirable copies made by Mr. Photis Zachariou, reproduced in my friend Professor Xyngopoulos' informative account of Pansellinos.

The Great Lavra. The monastery of the Great Lavra is the oldest, richest and most important on Athos. It is not, however, the most beautiful. Large as is the

area covered by its courtyard, it is not large enough comfortably to accommodate the quantity of buildings with which it is adorned and, while picturesque corners abound, the total effect is jumbled and confused. The *katholikon*, dedicated to the Dormition of the Virgin, is the model for almost all the churches on the Mountain, a domed cross-in-square with round apses on the cross-arms, a polygonal apse on the east and a domed narthex and exo-narthex on the west. Whether or not due to the efforts of those responsible for the rebuilding to prevent any repetition of the disaster which overwhelmed the founder, the dome seems almost too solid and the overall proportions clumsy. It is painted blood-red without, and within is covered with murals by the celebrated Cretan painter Theophanes dating from the 10th century. Whether, as some maintain, these have remained untouched since they were painted, or, as Robert Byron claimed, were heavily restored in the 18th century, they have certainly not been cleaned for a very long time. As the Cretan school habitually employed a far more sombre range of colours than the Macedonian, relying on a technique of carefully spaced highlights on a very dark under-painting, the total effect is one of gorgeous gloom in which details are hard to distinguish. The finest single scene, as I remember, is that of the Transfiguration. The exo-narthex was rebuilt early in the 19th century and later enlivened with the existing frescoes, usually dismissed as beneath contempt, but which include some little landscape panels in an almost Braque-like range of blacks, umbers and venetian red, which may be only folk-art but possess undoubted charm. Adjoining the main church are two chapels, one dedicated to the Forty Martyrs, the other to St. Nicholas; the former marks the spot where St. Athanasios suffered his fatal accident, the latter is decorated, rather prettily, with murals by another Cretan painter, Frangopoulos.

Of the rest of the various buildings enclosed in the great courtyard the most remarkable is the refectory opposite the *katholikon*. A cruciform building with an apse to accommodate the abbot's seat at the head of the cross, a splendid wooden roof and completely frescoed walls, it was built, or rather rebuilt, in the 16th century by Archbishop Gennadios of Serres. The best of the paintings are the entombment of Athanasios, a splendidly composed scene on a big scale, and a terrifying Doom of which the layout recalls that at Torcello, although it is far less accomplished, is in painting, not mosaic, and is nearly three centuries later in date. But finally, it is not any individual scene which remains in the mind so much as the completeness and consistency of the whole achievement, suggesting, as it does, a setting from some sumptuous production of *Boris Godunov*. Owing to the fact that the Lavra has long since abandoned the coenobitic rule for the idiorhythmic, whereby the monks are allowed to take their meals in their own cells, it now seldom fulfils its original function.

Between the refectory and the church stands the *phiale*, perhaps the most beautiful of any on Athos. The basin is enclosed by a series of marble slabs, carved with the usual Byzantine motifs, and covered by a Turkish style dome resting on a ring of pillars with elaborate capitals; it is flanked by two immensely old cypresses, said to have been planted by St. Athanasios and his companion St. Euthymios, one of which, when last I saw it, was going rapidly home.

Dionysiou. Not only is this the most beautifully situated of all the Athonite monasteries—perched on a high, impregnable rock overlooking the sea, its balconies and domes airborne on massive stone towers—but the one which most powerfully radiates an atmosphere of serenity and devotion. The abbot, when I was there, was a personage of great dignity and exceptional intelligence; not only was he fully aware of the value, both religious and aesthetic, of his house's treasures, but was possessed of a truly oecumenical spirit nourished by close contacts with All Saints', Margaret Street. The librarian was young, enthusiastic and had extremely clean hands, the food was plain but good and all the monks we met took a modest, unboastful pride in their monastery, such as one rarely encounters in the idiorhythmic houses.

Owing to the narrowness of the site there is here no vast courtyard with free-standing buildings, but a highly picturesque ecclesiastical warren on several levels. Founded towards the end of the 14th century by one of the Greek Emperors of Trebizond, the monastery fortunately escaped those devastating fires which regularly ravaged so many of its rivals and, until very recently when, to judge from photographs, a rather unfortunate concrete extension was added to one corner, had suffered comparatively little reconstruction. The church follows the usual plan, with additional domes over the *prothesis* and *diakonikon*, and is painted the familiar sang-de-bœuf in striking contrast to the adjacent arcaded passages (sometimes improperly referred to as cloisters) which are a very brilliant burnt orange. Inside there are paintings by another Cretan named Zorzi, rather lighter in tone and a great deal cleaner than those in the Lavra. There is also a T-shaped refectory frescoed with saints and martyrdoms which, as Dionysiou has never abandoned the coenobitic rule, is in regular use. On the back wall of the passage leading to it is an elaborate Doom wherein one of the devils is emitting an unquestionably mushroom-shaped cloud. The abbot, who carefully drew our attention

73

to it, regarded this as a clear warning of the coming nuclear holocaust in which most of the civilised world would be destroyed, but from which the Holy Mountain had been assured of Divine Protection. This cheerful conclusion provoked a pitying smile and a withering German comment on the abbot's credulity from the insufferable Lutheran student who had attached himself to us; personally I had an uneasy feeling that the good man might well be on to something.

Of the carefully preserved treasures the most beautiful is a superb Imperial chrysobul establishing and guaranteeing the monastery's foundation, one of the great masterpieces of Byzantine illumination; the most fascinating, a tusk of that strangest of all Orthodox saints, S. Cristophoros Cynocephalos, the dog-headed St. Christopher, a young man of exceptional physical beauty who, fearing lest he should prove a standing temptation to both sexes, prayed for, and was granted, this alarming transformation.

Vatopedi. Seen from afar Vatopedi has the appearance of some enormous fortified manor house, or possibly a small town, with little to suggest its religious character. From the tiny harbour a path winds upwards to a large

gateway, rather incongruously decorated with some unfortunate coloured glass, from which a strategically planned tunnel leads into one of the most extraordinary open spaces in the world.

'The irregular enclosure in which we now found ourselves covered an area of perhaps a couple of acres. The ground rose sharply on one side giving to that section of the encompassing wall and its adjoining buildings a cliff-like height, the effect of which had been artificially emphasised by setting the cobblestones in a great radiating arc, diminishing in numbers with the gradient, which recalled, although there the device is employed, as it were, in the reverse direction, the Piazza della Signoria in Siena. That, at first glance, was all that I was able distinctly to take in. The rest was a great, jumbled impression, quite staggering in its impact, of domes and arches, of ill-supported balconies projecting at improbable angles and perilous heights, of stone ramps and outside staircases, of free-standing churches in shocking-pink and wide-eaved, spiky-roofed clock-towers and, right at the far end, closing the vista, of a huge, arcaded, many-domed building freshly painted a vivid sang-de-bœuf. The only structure which even remotely suggested the non-Byzantine world, although without striking any jarring note of direct incongruity, was a large, many-storeyed, greystone block, immediately to our right, in a tolerably correct version of neo-classic with pilasters and pediments but saved from any hint of academicism by the bold use of white plastered pointing and the liberal application of light Prussian blue to mouldings and surrounds.'[1]

Vatopedi, although second to the Great Lavra in monastic precedence, is the largest of all the monasteries, among which it occupies a socially pre-dominant position analogous to that of Christ Church among the colleges of Oxford. Discounting improbable stories that connect it with the 5th-century Empress Pulcheria, its foundation came immediately after that of the Lavra at the end of the 10th century. The church, which is dedicated to the Annunciation, is a larger, more skilful version of that at the Lavra, and architecturally the finest on the Mountain. Painted sang-de-bœuf, the exterior is animated by the eye of God in a triangle in the centre of the façade, gazing down with, in these surroundings, a strangely Protestant, almost Masonic, fixity.

The interior, which is splendidly proportioned on the grandest scale, is completely covered with paintings of the Macedonian school, contemporary with those in the Protaton, but the majority repainted in the 18th century.

[1] *The Cornhill Magazine*, Spring 1958.

Personally I find the enthusiasm they aroused in the late Robert Byron, who held that they were the supreme masterpiece of that school, hard to share; grandly conceived and competently carried out, in their present condition they seem to me to be constricted by a certain academicism. However, this may well be due to the 18th-century restorers, for it is notable that the paintings in the exo-narthex, which, so it is maintained, have never been repainted, are far lighter in tone and consciously monumental in treatment than the rest, approximating more closely to contemporary work in the Protaton.

Grand and splendid as is the existing decoration, it may well have fallen short of the original intention of the founders. Over the entrance from the narthex into the main body of the church are some splendid mosaics in lunettes. Whether they are all that remain of the original scheme, or whether for some reason that scheme was abandoned in favour of fresco before it had been carried further, is not clear; various dates, ranging from the 11th to the

14th century, have been suggested but the earlier would appear to be the more likely.

The collection of relics and treasures housed at Vatopedi has long been the envy of all the other houses on Athos, including as it does the Virgin's girdle and a large fragment of the True Cross. From a purely aesthetic point of view the most rewarding are some icons, donated by the Iconodule Empress Theodora (possibly those which, as related in the well-known anecdote, the court-dwarf reported to her iconoclast husband she was hiding); some very beautiful, if alarmingly painstaking, portable mosaics; and a porphyry cup donated by the Despot of Epirus which has been accorded extravagant admiration by Western pilgrims. But for me the high-water mark among all these minor masterpieces is achieved by a series of small gold panels, embossed with the figures of saints, which have been incorporated into the frame of a reliquary; dating, I imagine, from the 9th or 10th century they are exquisite without being precious, monumental although miniature, supreme examples of a craft of which the Byzantines were always masters.

Other buildings in the great courtyard include sixteen churches (so it is claimed, but I have never counted), a fine 15th-century clock-tower, the oldest on the Mountain, and an elaborate *phiale*, the canopy of which is supported on a ring of coupled columns. The refectory was completely and very dully frescoed in the 18th century which also saw the erection of the ruined theological college outside the walls.

4

CONSTANTINOPLE

'SAILING to Byzantium' today may well generate feelings of enthusiasm and expectancy that are unlikely to survive arrival. The skyline, seen from the Marmora, remains one of the wonders of the world, but closer acquaintance reveals that it is that of a beautifully situated slum which is rapidly losing even the irrational justification of picturesqueness. The great monuments are still happily there, dominating an urban landscape bisected by permanently unfinished boulevards, dotted by mini-skyscrapers, knotted with traffic blocks and pitted by goods-yards and shanty-towns. Pylons bestride the Bosphorus, from the shores of which the old wooden *yalies* are vanishing one by one, and transistors drown the lapping of the Sweet Waters of Asia. The climate is deplorable and the communications are bad.

Of the less than a score of Byzantine churches which survive many are so ruinous or so altered as only to be of interest to the expert; some are mosques, some are museums, some appear to be permanently locked. Many are almost inaccessible, all, with two exceptions, demand the greatest pertinacity and a keen sense of direction on the part of the would-be visitor. However, of those that are closed to the public it is only fair to add that a high proportion are, at the moment, undergoing much needed repairs, in some cases just in time. Such secular monuments as have survived are more easily attainable, but it must be admitted that they are not, for the most part, of overwhelming beauty or outstanding significance.

The Pillar of Constantine. Of Constantine's city this is almost the only vestige remaining above ground. It stands where the Mesé, the principal artery of Byzantium, which followed approximately the same line as the Bayazit Boulevard, crossed the second forum. Calcined by innumerable fires, cracked by earthquakes and kept together by iron bands, it is remarkable only for its survival. It was once crowned by an enormous statue of the Emperor in gilded bronze, said to have been originally a statue of Apollo by Phidias transformed by a few deft touches into a likeness of the Thirteenth Apostle, (a process which recalls the late Sir Edwin Lutyens' prompt reply when asked, after the First World War, how much it would cost to convert the Duke of York's column into a memorial to Lord Kitchener: 'Five bob— half-a-crown for each moustache!'). This composite masterpiece finally collapsed in the 12th century when it was replaced by a great golden cross.

The Aqueduct of Valens. A good straightforward example of Roman engineering built some time during the reign (364–378) of the unfortunate Emperor whose name it bears, bestriding the Ataturk Boulevard. While it cannot be claimed that it possesses the monumental quality of the Aqueduct at Segovia, or achieves the dramatic effect of the Pont du Gard, it is good, functional architecture which fulfilled its purpose, that of keeping the innumerable cisterns in all quarters of the city well supplied, for centuries. Some of these cisterns, of which the most remarkable is that built by Justinian and known as the 'Thousand and One Columns', may, not without difficulty, be visited by those keenly interested in hydraulics.

The Hippodrome. The scene of so much excitement and bloodshed today lies several feet below the level of a mournful public garden to the south of Hagia Sophia. It is, however, still possible to trace the line of the 'Spina', the long, narrow platform running down the centre of the track, by the surviving monuments. Of these the length of twisted green copper in the middle is the most romantic, the Egyptian obelisk to the north the most interesting. The former is all that remains of the great column formed of three intertwined serpents supporting a golden tripod erected on the Sacred Way at Delphi to commemorate the victory of Plataea; the latter, which was commissioned by Thothmes III, was brought from Karnak and set up in its present position by order of Theodosius I in the year 390. The Obelisk itself, although rather better preserved, is of no greater interest than those on the Victoria Embankment and the Place de la Concorde, but the base on which it is set is fascinating and merits careful inspection. On all four sides are groups of the Imperial family attending various functions in the Hippodrome—opening the games, prize-giving, etc. Not only do they provide valuable evidence of the construction of the Kathisma (or Imperial Box) which stood roughly on the site now occupied by the Kaiser's hideous little presentation fountain, but also of the appearance of various contemporaries, as the carvings are almost certainly portraits carried out during their subjects' lifetime; stylistic-ally they mark the very moment when the slick illusionism of late Hellenistic sculpture was giving way to that conceptual approach which was to dominate representational art, both in East and West, for the next thousand years.

Of all the other trophies which once adorned the Hippodrome—the statues of successful charioteers, the bronze horses of Lysippus brought from Rome by Theodosius II to decorate the Kathisma which have now, after careering over half Europe, finally come to rest on the façade of S. Marco—there remains only the battered obelisk of Constantine Porphyrogenitus, once sheathed in bronze.

The Great Palace. Of this extensive conglomeration of halls, porticoes, stoas and apartments, constantly being altered and added to, which once covered most of the area between the Mosque of Sultan Achmet and the Marmora, there are today but a few fragments of masonry of different dates, an occasional stretch of wall and a series of Mosaic pavements. These last are under cover in a well-signposted building called, rather grandly, the Mosaic Museum. About the dating of these pavements there has been a considerable difference of opinion; some scholars put them as early as the reign of Theodosius II, others would place them as late as the end of the 6th century; most, however, express an enthusiasm for their beauty that personally I find it impossible to share. The style is full-blown, late Roman Beaux-Arts, the subject-matter sentimental or carnivorous, the treatment spectacularly un-suitable for the decoration of a pavement. Hunters eviscerate game, and wild animals devour each other with a sadistic enthusiasm only matched by the sculpture in the Tuileries Gardens. Of the less bloodthirsty scenes the one which evokes the most general approval is that of a small boy feeding a donkey, of which Landseer himself would not have been ashamed. Tech-nically of the highest quality, these mosaics display none of the provincial directness and vitality which make so many of the North African pavements in the Bardo Museum in Tunis so enjoyable, and, as far as one can judge from photographs, are aesthetically inferior to those at Antioch.

The Theodosian Walls. In mediaeval times these were rightly considered an additional wonder of the world and today they still remain the most im-pressive extant example of military architecture. Rendered necessary by the rapid spread of the city in the century after Constantine, they were erected during the reign of Theodosius II, but it would seem highly unlikely that that unimaginative and weak-willed Emperor's personal contribution to the enterprise justified the permanent association of his name. Stretching from the sea of Marmora on the south, where they join up with the sea walls, to the Golden Horn on the north, a distance of four-and-a-half miles, pierced by six great gates and several posterns (one of them the Golden Gate, near the southern extremity, incorporating a triumphal arch erected on the city outskirts by Theodosius I), with ninety-six projecting towers each sixty feet high, this extraordinary rampart was completed in the incredibly short space of twelve months, an unparalleled triumph of well-directed panic. Less than forty years after completion almost the whole wall and over half the towers were thrown down by a disastrous earthquake just at the moment when Attila, the Scourge of God, was advancing rapidly through Thrace. Fortunately the Greeks were able to buy time, which they used to such good purpose that not only did they repair the wall in two months but also added the outer wall in front of it, complete with moat and towers. In the 12th century the northernmost stretch was rebuilt as a single line, bulging outwards, in order to incorporate the Blachernae Palace, of which nothing today remains, erected by the Emperor Manuel I as the new Imperial Residence, replacing Justinian's old palace on the Bosphorus.

Today the walls remain, considering all that has happened to them in the course of a millennium and a half, astonishingly well-preserved and immensely impressive. The new by-pass running alongside has successfully banished the air of steel-engraved remoteness which they still displayed even twenty years ago when only a track with some market gardens and maize plots separated these massive watch-towers from the vast emptiness of the Thracian plain. Not only are they remarkable in themselves but, thanks to the impression they made on Saracens and Crusaders alike, their influence on the military architecture of the Middle Ages was worldwide, and there is no mediaeval walled town from Cairo to Caernarvon that does not in some measure pay them the tribute of unconscious imitation. Here and there they have been pierced for new streets, and the process of gradual dissolution has only occasionally been checked by restoration, notably at the Adrianople Gate which has been largely rebuilt. Fairly tactfully done, the gleaming new stonework nevertheless poses an awkward question. How far can restoration safely go in the case of purely functional architecture which today serves no practical purpose whatever? Do nothing and in time it will crumble away: do too much and you achieve an unconvincing film-set such as Carcassonne. Where only fragments remain they can, with skill and taste, occasionally be incorporated in other buildings, as witness those sections of the Aurelian wall so successfully preserved in the Rome railway station, but with so vast a relic as the walls of Constantinople such a solution is manifestly impossible. Probably the best course is to check all structural decay, forbid any drastic demolition or remodelling and allow time to work its changes on the surface. Whether or not the Turks will have the energy to maintain it for themselves, or the strong-mindedness (which the Athenians so signally lacked in the case of the stoa) to turn down well-meaning American plans for reconstruction, remains to be seen.

The Monastery of S. John Studion. The oldest surviving church in the city and the only basilica, it is also the only one which can today properly be described as picturesque. Tucked away at the very extremity of the sea walls on the shore of the Marmora, in a dreary and unattractive neighbourhood of railway sidings and junkyards, there still clings to this roofless shrine, with its ruinous, overgrown *atrium*, an extraordinary air of melancholy and romance. Founded in 463, it once accommodated more than a thousand monks who maintained, by working shifts, a continuous celebration of the Divine Liturgy day and night, at least in their early pioneering days. Its connection with the Imperial Family, many of whom received their education here, was always close and at first happy. But during the Iconoclastic controversy it became increasingly embittered and the monks, headed by their greatest Abbot, Theodore of Studion, were in the vanguard of those defending images, suffering many casualties before the struggle was finally won.

Damaged on numerous occasions by fire and earthquakes, the church was lavishly restored in the 12th century and again under the Palaeologues; after the Conquest it was perverted into a mosque and was finally ruined in the great earthquake of 1894. Today there remains a nave, very wide and short by Western basilican standards, a large apse, partly Turkish work, six very beautiful pillars of *verde antico*, still so vividly green as to suggest malachite, supporting an architrave, above which formerly rose a gallery, and a splendid floor of *opus Alexandrinum* which probably dates from the last restoration. There is no *prothesis* or *diakonikon*, the aisles not terminating in side apses, and the circle of tiered seats round the main apse has long since vanished, as has the altar to which the Emperor Michael V so ineffectually clung when the mob were out for his blood. However, there is still a fine narthex, roofless but retaining a marble entablature, carried on Corinthian columns, of the very highest quality. Both the narthex and the church itself were roofed in wood. The *atrium*, in which there is still a fragmentary fountain for ablutions, is now an oddly moving tangle of weeds, flowering shrubs and Turkish tombs.

SS. Sergius and Bacchus (Kucuk Hagia Sophia). During the reign of his uncle and predecessor, Justinian became involved in some unfortunate intrigue which, being discovered, was likely to have cost him his life had not Saints Sergius and Bacchus intervened on his behalf by appearing to the Emperor in a dream. Ever grateful for supernatural assistance, one of his first acts on coming to the throne was to build this magnificent church, just outside the Palace walls, dedicated to his saviours. More accessible, but even more dismally situated than S. John Studion, right alongside the tracks, the church externally is today indistinguishable from a genuine mosque, so thoroughly was the 15th-century transformation carried out. Within, despite considerable efforts—coats of whitewash, fussy arabesques stencilled in Reckitt's blue, and worst of all, a false wooden floor high enough to cut off the bases of the piers and columns, so producing a maddening overall effect of squatness— Islam has not, thank heaven, succeeded in suppressing the building's original character.

One's first impression is of an almost carefree vitality, which may just possibly in part be due to the fact, only apparent on plan, that the builders, if not the architect, were playing it by ear. The piers are not properly aligned, the apse is way off centre, and the dome is hopelessly crooked. This encourages the belief, which many would deny, that it is a little earlier rather than a year later than S. Vitale with which, as has been already suggested, it has much in common. In both churches the central area is octagonal in plan, with piers and exedras, but here the latter are confined to the angles and the octagon is enclosed in a square. The dome, strictly speaking, is not a true dome but a vault with sixteen groins, alternately flat and concave, rising directly from the arches. The gallery is supported not on arcades but on an entablature which runs right round the nave and is only broken in front of the *bema*.

The interior was, we know, most sumptuously decorated, as befitted an Imperial foundation with direct access to the Palace, but no trace of glittering mosaics or of polished marbles has survived, and only the exceptional richness and elaboration of the carved capitals and architraves remain to indicate the high quality of this vanished grandeur. The capitals on the ground-level are of the so-called 'Melon' type, slightly ribbed and covered with a very deeply drilled and crisply cut all-over tracery of acanthus fronds, as fine as

83

any in Hagia Sophia or S. Vitale. Those in the gallery, although beautifully worked, are rather less satisfactory in design; the impost-block is so heavy that it appears to have squashed and flattened the highly unorthodox Ionic capital beneath. The entablature separating the two levels is particularly elaborate and magnificent, with a heavy cornice supported on delicately carved consoles, bands of egg-and-dart mouldings and acanthus leaves, and on the frieze a long and fulsome Latin inscription in praise of Justinian and the 'God-crowned Theodora whose mind is bright with piety'.

At one period, when ecclesiastical relations were rather more oecumenical than was usual, SS. Sergius and Bacchus, together with an adjacent basilica, were set aside for the benefit of those following the Latin rite, and it is likely that from time to time Mass was celebrated here by no less a figure than Pope Gregory the Great who was for a time the Nuncio.

S. Irene. This is the second largest church in the city and probably rests on the oldest foundations. The original structure was destroyed together with Hagia Sophia during the Nika riots; restored, it was again burnt down in 564; once more restored it was once more destroyed, this time by an earthquake, in 740. The present building is, therefore, a rather ham-fisted amalgam of three previous churches. It was originally, and in a modified form still is, basically, a basilica, but a basilica to which, probably in the first re-building, a dome was added over the easternmost bay of the nave. This was originally supported on four arches of which those on the north and south were later extended into barrel vaults through the supporting piers of which aisles were inserted; at the same time the western bay was also covered by a barrel vault, and a *Gynecaeum*, or women's enclosure, was added above the narthex on a level with the aisle galleries. Then, presumably after the earthquake, the western bay was covered by what might laughingly be described as a dome; in fact it is a highly unprofessional combination of vaults and pendentives looking rather as though it had been squeezed into shape out of plasticine and thickly whitewashed. Eastward the nave terminates in a great apse with, at its base, the original half-circle of tiered seats, technically known as a *synthronon*, of which an unusual feature is the enclosed ambulatory running beneath it, illuminated by small openings cut in the seats themselves. Above is a remnant of gold mosaic in the half-dome on which is emblazoned the simple cross which was all the Iconoclasts would allow by way of decoration. Judging from a Greek inscription running round the soffit of the arch immediately in front, it probably superseded an original Pantokrator.

S. Saviour in Chora, Constantinople

Externally the church is unremarkable. The eastern dome is enclosed by a low many-windowed drum; that on the west is too shallow to break the skyline. The northern and southern arms of the crossing, too unobtrusive to rank as transepts, are terminated by walls following the line of the vaulting and pierced by three rows of windows (five apiece in the two lower, three in the topmost) an arrangement very popular in Constantinople. On the west is a narthex of five bays, three domed, two cross-vaulted, now approached from the north by a long descending ramp from the present day ground-level. Beyond is an *atrium*, still with its enclosing arcades, although these are largely Turkish work, the only one in the city, apart from the tangled little garth of S. John Studion.

S. Irene, incidentally, is the only church in Constantinople, except S. Mary of the Mongols down in the Phanar, never at any time to have been a mosque (until quite recently it was a military museum into which no one was able to penetrate). Although not, perhaps, outstandingly beautiful, it is of the greatest interest architecturally for the light it throws on the principal problem which Byzantine architects of this period had set themselves. This was how best to combine the central plan of such churches as S. Vitale and SS. Sergius and Bacchus with that of the traditional basilica in order to provide the maximum space. At S. Irene they were on the brink of a solution; add domed transepts on the north and south and you have a crossed domed basilica such as the Holy Apostles and S. Marco; add supporting half-domes to east and west and you have, approximately, Hagia Sophia.

S. Irene has one further distinction; alone among the city churches, apart from Hagia Sophia, it is reasonably easy to find. Unaccompanied females, however, should be warned that the dim galleries above the aisles are a favourite lurking place for the soldiery from the nearby barracks, who may not be brutal but are certainly licentious.

Hagia Sophia. More justly, perhaps, than any other building in the world can the Church of the Divine Wisdom be described as miraculous. It was a miracle that it was successfully built and an even greater miracle that it stayed up. The man chiefly responsible, Anthemios of Tralles, was not an architect but a professor of solid geometry with, so far as we know, no building experience whatever. (His partner, Isidore of Miletus, had, it is true, written a treatise on vaulting, but is chiefly known as a commentator on Euclid.) The construction of this extraordinary building, therefore, represents the practical application of an elaborate theory worked out on paper and, as a purely intellectual feat, may be compared with that of the late Lord Cherwell who, it is said, during the first war produced a mathematical formula for getting aircraft out of spins and then took up an airplane and proved it. It remains a unique achievement, for never before and never afterwards did the Byzantines build a church approaching it in size or rivalling it in boldness.

Roughly speaking the plan consists of a square, 100 ft. × 100 ft., enclosed in a rectangle, 250 ft. × 255 ft., covered by a shallow dome on pendentives supported by four enormous piers with half-domes opening to east and west surmounting two pairs of exedra, the whole area linked by cross-vaults and arcades to the walls of the surrounding rectangle. However, structurally nothing here is quite what it seems, and few buildings of this importance can afford so little satisfaction to the doctrinaire advocates of truth in architecture. Although the half-domes appear to be buttressing the main dome on the east and west, they in fact receive very little of the thrust; the aisles and galleries, which give the effect of supporting the central area, are completely detached, their function purely scenic. But Anthemios, it soon became apparent, had been too daring by half and Justinian too impatient. (The whole building was completed in the incredibly short time of five years, ten months.) The original dome collapsed in 558 when it was discovered that, during the twenty years it had been in position, its weight, despite the fact that it was constructed of specially baked lightweight bricks, had caused the piers and buttresses to tip backward and the arches to expand. The present dome with which Isidore's nephew replaced it was raised in height and is borne on forty ribs, with the same number of windows between them, supported on the outside by small buttresses producing the effect of a low drum. At the same time the pier-arches were widened and the lateral walls strengthened. This, however, was not the end of the story; the western half of the new dome came down in 989 and the eastern portion in 1346. On both occasions it was successfully repaired but at some time or other, probably in the 9th century, two pairs of enormous buttresses had to be added on the north and south, which had themselves later to be further weighed down and anchored by the imposition of the existing turrets.

Having determined on so stupendous a structure, Justinian was naturally not prepared to stint on the decoration. From all over the Empire came shiploads of marble—porphyry and *verde antico*, Istrian and Pentelic; stone-masons, mosaicists, sculptors, carpenters, bricklayers, plasterers, all worked overtime. To finance this vast project, the whole economy of the city was upset; salaries went unpaid and schools remained empty in order to meet the staggering cost, some seventy million pounds sterling at present rates. However, the popular theory that such great buildings of antiquity as the temple of Diana at Ephesus and the temples of Baalbek were ransacked for rare columns seems unlikely to be true, as distinct traces of contemporary quarrying have been discovered as far away as the First Cataract.

Over-excited by the copy-writer's pages of Paul the Silentiary and Procopius, the modern visitor, expectant of spectacular lavishness, may perhaps be slightly disappointed, on entering the main body of the church through the Royal door, by the absence of glitter, although he can hardly fail to be overwhelmed by the sudden revelation of such spatial grandeur. The few remaining mosaics are not immediately visible; the marble revetment and innumerable columns look as though they had not been polished for centuries, which is probably the case; the great marble ambo, the solid silver iconostasis, the myriad gold lamps have all long since vanished. Only the superb quality of the carved capitals and string-courses, as fresh and crisp as the day they were cut, have come down to us unimpaired.

Of the remaining mosaics, that of the Virgin and Child with a fragmentary archangel in the half-dome over the apse, is sometimes claimed as the earliest, dating from the 9th century, but some authorities would place it as late as the 13th. Not easy to see, it is well worth the trouble of taking field-glasses, as the head of the angel is, to my mind, the most beautiful mosaic in the whole church. In the great narthex, itself the size of a small basilica, are traces of some very beautiful pattern-work in the southern bays, which may conceivably be the only remaining fragments of Justinian's original decoration, and two lunettes. The first, over the south entrance, showing Constantine and Justinian respectively offering models of the City and the Church to the Virgin, dates from the end of the 10th century; that over the main door in which a very Armenian-looking Emperor, probably Leo VI, prostrates himself before Our Lord, is a work of the 9th or early 10th.

In the gallery (which is not always open but which should on no account be missed) are two pairs of portrait panels, one of John II Comnenus and his *backfisch* wife on either side of Christ; the other of the Empress Zoe and an Emperor whose head would seem to have been altered from time to time in order to conform to the features of her current husband. Also here is a magnificent Deesis, Our Lord between the Virgin and the Baptist, about the exact date of which there is considerable argument. Some would place it a short time after the Latin interregnum, others claim that it was installed immediately prior to that disaster. However, whatever its exact date, it is a work of quite exceptional delicacy and refinement which many consider to be one of the supreme achievements of Byzantine art. Personally, while readily acknowledging its extraordinary accomplishment, I find the refinement almost obtrusive and the delicacy so stressed as to come within measurable distance of softness.

Almost the first act of Mehmet the Conqueror was to turn the Great Church into a mosque, which was a disaster; almost exactly five hundred years later Kemal Ataturk converted it into a museum, which was a greater disaster. The slight change of function involved in the former metamorphosis, although unfortunate, was not lethal, but the complete suspension of function imposed by its present status is the kiss of death; it is far better for the House of God to fall into the hands of the Infidel than to pass into the custody of the Office of Works. Almost all the changes involved in this second transformation were unfortunate; the great green discs bearing Koranic texts which formerly hung free from the roof when, to judge from old prints, they served to emphasise the vastness of the interior, were taken down and replaced flat against the walls, where they ruin the lines of the architecture and, in one case at least, completely mask a mosaic panel; the Sultan's box, pretty enough in itself, seems lost and pointless without the surrounding prayer rugs and carpets slanted towards Mecca; and now the bronze hoops which held the mosque-lamps are being tarted up with the cheapest gold paint to glitter distractingly just above eye-level.

Today no great building in the world is so completely lacking in atmosphere as Hagia Sophia. The impression it creates upon the beholder is purely architectural, reinforced by no emotional or picturesque side-effects. But thanks to the genius of Anthemios and Isidore we do not feel the lack, for if, as I believe, architecture is primarily the art of manipulating space, the Church of the Holy Wisdom unquestionably remains one of the supreme examples.

S. Mary Diaconissa (*Kalenderhane Djami*). Everything about this church is extremely vague, including the name. It now seems likely that it is not, in fact, S. Mary Diaconissa at all but the church of the monastery of Christ Akataleptos. Some say it is a building of the 9th century, others, who detect a resemblance to a church at Caryes on Mount Athos, that it dates from the 10th. The central core, which is all that remains of the original structure, is a Greek cross on plan surmounted by a dome. There are traces of aisles, and the chambers in the angles of the cross may once have supported domes,

which would make the church one of the earliest examples of this type of layout. The narthex and exo-narthex are both of later date and the apse vanished when the church became a mosque. Inside it is said to retain fragments of the original marble revetment, but as it is closed for restoration and heavily barricaded with barbed-wire these must, at the moment, be taken on trust.

The Palace of Constantine Porphyrogenitus (Tekfursaray). This melancholy façade, adjacent to the Theodosian wall, was probably built, not by the Emperor whose name it bears, but by Manuel I in the middle of the 12th century. Almost the sole existing example of Byzantine secular architecture, it does much to reconcile us to the disappearance of all the rest. At first glance it might easily be taken for an unfortunate essay in 19th-century *rundbogenstil*; the fenestration is clumsy, the decoration, contrasting stripes of stone and brick relieved with chequer-work, fussy. When one thinks of such contemporary buildings as the Doges' Palace, or the *municipio* at Piacenza, which are composed of much the same elements, one realises how shaky was the Byzantine architects' grasp of proportion when confronted with the flat expanse of a façade. The truth is that Byzantine architecture was essentially theocentric; lacking the religious impulse and the restraint imposed by dogma, inspiration withered away.

S. Theodosia (*Gul Djami or Rose Mosque*). As seen by the camera this is a towering, nobly proportioned, dome-crowned church, but a close investigation of the photographs reveals that they have almost invariably been taken with a telescopic lens. To the naked eye the dome is invisible and the structure incomprehensible due to the close proximity of adjacent buildings. However, it is just possible to get some idea of the beauty of the three apses, elaborately niched, from a nearby knacker's yard infested by a particularly savage dog. And this, practically speaking, is all, for although it was said quite recently to be still functioning as a mosque it is now, although much dilapidated, firmly closed and the key unobtainable. The interior, according to all accounts, was almost entirely rebuilt in Turkish times, although the original massive piers, which now support pointed arches, are still in place. Under one of them, according to a tradition which has apparently absolutely nothing to support it, lies the body of the last Emperor, Constantine Palaeologus.

S. Saviour (*Pantokrator*). Unlike most of the Constantinople churches, this is nobly sited and visible from afar, which does not, however, make it any easier to find, for once one has crossed the Ataturk bridge it drops below the sky-line and proves attainable only after endless twistings and false starts through the maze of ancient, rubble-filled alleys that surround it. Once reached, it turns out to be not one church but three. That on the north is a small cross-in-square built in the 10th century; next to it is a small funerary chapel with domes over the *naos* and *bema* of a slightly later date; beyond this to the south is a rather larger church, also cross-in-square in plan, with pillars, not piers, supporting the dome, that was built in the 12th century by the Empress Irene. All three churches have a single connecting narthex but that on the south is also provided with an exo-narthex projecting beyond the façade. The two outermost churches have three apses apiece, the chapel in the middle only one.

In Imperial times this was one of the most important religious foundations in the city. Irene added to it a monastery, and her husband the Emperor John II, who died as a result of a hunting accident in Cilicia, was buried here; the whole enterprise was probably finished by their son, Manuel I, whose first wife was interred in the funerary chapel. This sovereign also added to the extensive collection of relics (which included a piece of the True Cross) the celebrated Icon of S. Demetrios which he obtained by an enforced

exchange from the Great Basilica in Thessaloniki. During the Latin occupation all these were pillaged and the True Cross ended up in Alsace.

Some years ago the church, which had been serving as a mosque for centuries, was secularised and is destined to become a museum. At the moment of writing, restoration is theoretically going on, and the interior can only be glimpsed by diving under barriers and squinting through windows.

The Theotokos Pammakaristos (Fethiye Djami). The church of the All-Blessed Mother of God is a double one; to the original building, which dates from the beginning of the 12th century, was added in the 14th a *parekklesion*, by a lady with the high-sounding name of Maria Ducaena Comnena Palaeologina, to serve as a funerary chapel for her husband, which she adorned with a moving inscription expressive of her grief. Formerly there was also a monastery the abbot of which exercised considerable influence during the

Commene period. After the Turkish conquest it became the seat of the Patriarch who remained here until it was turned into a mosque in 1586.

The earlier church has a large central dome on a high drum pierced with twelve recessed windows separated by twelve engaged columns, an arrangement very typical of the period. The rather dull interior is devoid of decoration and has not been improved by the substitution at the east end of an asymmetrical, Mecca-orientated triangle for the original apse. Beneath a flagstone in the south aisle is the entrance to an underground passage, for

which the guardian makes the improbable claim that it leads direct to Hagia Sophia, a couple of hills away. The *parekklesion* has three nicely grouped little domes and is elaborately decorated externally in a style which evokes much admiration. Personally I find that the combination of round-headed windows, chequer-work, niches and blind-arcading with parti-coloured stripes suggests an unholy alliance between Fabergé and Butterfield. Inside there are splendid mosaics including, to judge from the reproductions, a magnificent Pantokrator in the main dome. If you can get in to see them you will be very, very lucky.

Immediately alongside the church is a modern infants' school, and care should be taken that visits do not coincide with the breaks, which are numerous and long.

S. Saviour in Chora (Kahriye Djami). As the name indicates ('in the Fields') this church originally stood outside the city and was founded, therefore, before the erection of the Theodosian walls. Of the earliest church and of that with which Justinian replaced it, we know nothing save that the latter, by the end of the Iconoclastic Controversy, was in ruins, and was entirely rebuilt. The main structure of the present church probably represents this rebuilding. After the Latin occupation it was once more ruinous and was restored by Theodore Metochites, the Grand Logothete, who is depicted, wearing an enormous turban, offering the church to Christ in one of the lunettes; he it was who added the exo-narthex, the *parekklesion* and all the exquisite decoration. (The date, 1303, which some claim to have deciphered in one of the mosaics, remains dubious.)

The church is Greek-cross in plan with exceptionally short arms that do not project beyond the side walls, and a large apse flanked by a *prothesis* and *diakonikon* having no direct communication with the *naos*. The mosaics in the main church, except for a Dormition of the Virgin on the west and two icons on the side walls, have vanished, but the marble revetment and the carved cornices, all of the greatest beauty, remain intact. But the principal glory of the church rests on the wonderful series of mosaics and paintings in the narthex and *parekklesion*. That S. Saviour had been particularly richly decorated had long been known (there are fragmentary sketches in Van Milligen's book published in 1912), but the extent and quality of the adornment was only revealed in very recent years by the painstaking work of American Byzantinists. In the exo-narthex are scenes from the life of Christ which at first glance seem to be, but probably are not, rather arbitrarily arranged; those in the inner narthex illustrate the apochryphal life of the Virgin Mary. Both series exhibit a liveliness of conception and a delicacy of treatment that are quite new; delightful and fantastic architectural features are linked to each other by trailing curtains, tree-fringed hillocks stand out like theatrical ground-rows against a golden sky, the principal events are witnessed by clusters of animated and keenly interested spectators and ignored by beautifully observed animals and birds. The artist, or artists, responsible shared with those working in the narthex of S. Marco a narrative gift seldom displayed by their forerunners during the Middle Byzantine period.

The *parekklesion*, which is covered by two domes, that to the west on a drum, the other much shallower, is dominated by the great painting of the Anastasis in the apse. Like the 'Burial of Count Orgaz' and the 'View of Delft' this is one of the world's great pictures which achieve an effect on first sight for which no amount of study, however prolonged, of reproductions, however good, will have prepared the beholder. The strength and vigour with which Christ hauls up our first parents from the grave; the sense of speed and rush conveyed by the figure of Adam; the general feeling of urgency created by the disposal of the various groups; all combine not only

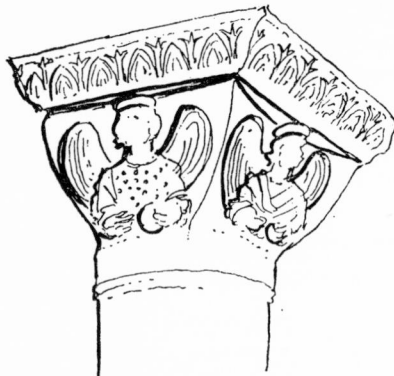

to make this, quite apart from the beauty of the colour, the supreme, if perhaps uncharacteristic, masterpiece of Byzantine art but to raise it to the universal class. Indeed, if asked to name the greatest single example of Christian iconography, I would hesitate between this and Piero della Francesca's 'Resurrection' at Borgo San Sepolcro. The remaining paintings in the chapel, if comparatively conventional, are not unworthy.

Until recently it was customary to discover in these works, both mosaics and paintings, a reflection of what was going on in contemporary Florence; personally I get no hint of Italian influence. Only the carvings of the borders round the funerary niches in the *parekklesion* and the icon frame in the main church display some faint, and almost certainly superficial, suggestion of Western contacts. The curious and very beautiful capitals of the pillars in the ante-chamber are certainly unique in Byzantine architecture, but any faint resemblance to Gothic or Romanesque models I should judge to be fortuitous.

5

GREECE, SOUTH OF THE PINDUS

EVEN during the hey-day of the Roman Empire, Greece was to be accounted one of the more depressed provinces. Regularly exploited by a succession of corrupt and rapacious governors, producing nothing, except antiques, that the Romans could not more easily get elsewhere, what prosperity it enjoyed was largely due, as in later times, to the tourist trade. Wealthy Philhellenes such as Herodes Atticus and the Emperor Hadrian proclaimed their culture by the erection of monuments, and the University by the Ilissos continued to attract foreign students until it was finally closed by the Emperor Justinian. But such benefits were largely confined to Athens; elsewhere the slackening of the tempo of Hellenic life was only seasonally quickened at Olympia and Delphi which continued for a time to attract a steadily diminishing number of pilgrims and athletes.

The establishment of Christianity and the removal of the Capital eastwards did not immediately have the tonic effect that might have been expected. The Athenians, as St. Paul had discovered, were intelligent but sceptical, and the country folk remained obstinately attached to their old beliefs. (In the southern Peloponnese, paganism was not finally suppressed until the 9th century, and then so superficially that even today survivals of the old faith are clearly and frequently apparent beneath the top dressing of Orthodoxy.)

In addition, Byzantium, although comparatively close at hand, was soon beset by its own troubles and could at first afford scant protection to such outlying and not very important territories. So, during the early years of the Eastern Empire, Greece was regularly ravaged by Goths, Bulgarians and Avars, and steadily penetrated by Slavs. Nevertheless, during the 5th and 6th centuries, churches of a considerable size were erected, almost all in coastal towns. All of these have long since vanished, but the foundations of three are still clearly visible—at Nea Anchialos on the coast of Thessaly, at Corinth, and at Vraona on the Attic coast, alongside a very ancient shrine where

Artemis had formally been worshipped in the form of a she-bear. All were large basilicas with double aisles and, probably, galleries. But for two reasons the prosperity of these seaports was short-lived; first, the fact that the Aegean archipelago provided an ideal stamping ground for a steadily increasing number of infidel sea-raiders, and second, the rapid growth in wealth and importance of the great Macedonian city of Thessaloniki, through which trade with the Balkan hinterland and central Europe was now channelled direct to Constantinople.

That Greece today, despite such unpromising beginnings, can boast more Byzantine churches than any other part of the Empire is almost entirely due to that great Emperor Basil II Bulgaroktonos (Bulgar-Slayer). Not only did his successful prosecution of the activities which got him his name assure the country a security such as it had not enjoyed for years, but he also cultivated an enlightened and practical Philhellenism, remarkable and unexpected in so dour and ascetic a character. On the occasion of his visit to Greece, after the successful termination of his Bulgarian campaigns in 1019, not content with redecorating in the most lavish style the second largest church in Christendom, 'that Pagans call the Parthenon' (a few faint traces of saints' heads in roundels on the western wall of the *cella* still testify to the imperial beneficence), he launched and encouraged a great wave of church-building which was to continue unabated until the time of the Latin Conquest.

After this disaster most of the country remained in Frankish or Venetian hands until the coming of the Turks, for the Emperor, notwithstanding he soon recovered his capital, was never able to re-establish his sway over most of the provinces. However, exceptions there were of which the principal was the central Peloponnese, dominated by the great mountain stronghold of Mistra, overlooking Sparta, which, after the expulsion of the Norman family of Villehardouin, became the last flourishing centre of Byzantine culture.

The coming of the Turks put an end to any further church-building on an extensive scale. Not that the Ottomans made any attempt either to suppress or convert; on the contrary, as their subjects were divided according to their beliefs, not their nationalities, and administered through their own religious authorities, the Church enjoyed an increased, if less spiritual, influence, but, on the one hand, any unusual expenditure would inevitably attract the tax-gatherer, and on the other, the steady decline of the population obviated the need for any new places of worship. Such churches as were built were usually small and rustic variations on the cross-in-square plan, or else plain barrel-vaulted halls with a projecting apse. But if the days of architectural experiment were long since past, interior decoration continued (and unfortunately still does) and the majority of wall-paintings throughout Greece date, anyhow in their present visible state, from after the Conquest. At the same time the decorative impulse of the peasantry found a beguiling outlet in the carving and gilding of the wooden iconostases which now came largely to replace the older examples in stone. The results, in which the locals take an enormous pride, are frequently of a manic complexity hardly to be surpassed by the niggling genius of the Swiss or the Japanese.

Of the vast number of remaining churches it would be manifestly impossible to deal with more than a small proportion in the following pages, even were my knowledge far more extensive than it is. I have therefore confined myself, apart from those of great historical or aesthetic importance, to such as are both typical and reasonably accessible. To any reader infuriated by the omission of some personal favourite I herewith offer my humble apologies.

ATHENS

Compared to such cities as Alexandria, Antioch or Ephesus, Athens was never in Hellenistic times a large centre of population, and as the years went by the number of its inhabitants steadily decreased. It is not necessary, therefore, to explain the extreme smallness of the existing churches, as is frequently done, on the grounds of poverty; with two such places of worship as the Parthenon and the Theseion (the church of S. George in Byzantine times) Athenian congregational needs were more than adequately met, and the new churches were in most cases concrete expressions of personal piety rather than machines for public worship.

The Church of the Holy Apostles. Discounting the fragments of an early basilica incorporated in the Stoa of Attalus, and the foundations of another which, before recent road works, were alleged, but not by me, to be visible alongside the Ilissos, this is the oldest church in Athens. Formerly situated in the most crowded part of the old town, it now stands on the edge of the denuded Agora, mercifully spared, and, indeed, tactfully restored, by transatlantic zeal. Basically cruciform, all the arms of the cross (in the case of the western arm, only internally) terminate in apses, a type of plan known as quatrefoil which one school of historians obsessively attribute to Armenian influence. Although comparatively rare in this part of the world it occurs frequently

97

on Mount Athos, probably because it was liturgically well suited to monastic churches where considerably larger numbers of worshippers would have regularly to be accommodated in the *naos*. Erected in the early 11th century on the site of an earlier church, which may have replaced a still more ancient baptistry, the main fabric as it exists today is a careful work of restoration carried out by American Byzantinists whose aim was to approximate as closely as possible to its original condition. That the whole plan of the church had been basically changed in the intervening centuries is suggested by the entry in the 1900 edition of Murray's Handbook (singularly well-informed on Byzantine buildings, considering the date) which describes the east end as terminating in a square apse. More recently, the wall-paintings, which are said to be fine, have been carefully uncovered and restored.

The Little Metropolis. Originally dedicated to S. Eleftherios, this charming little church got its familiar name from the proximity of the modern cathedral. (This monstrous building was designed in the middle of the last century by four singularly untalented architects and largely constructed, it is said, of rubble taken from no less than seventy demolished churches.) A typical example of the cross-in-square plan, its distinction chiefly lies in the exterior decoration. In all the walls, of Pentelic marble which has weathered to a wonderful rust-red, are embedded Byzantine engraved slabs, ancient inscriptions, signs of the zodiac, Frankish escutcheons and lengths of classical entablatures. Superior persons used pompously to claim that this apparently haphazard use of an antique bric-a-brac clearly demonstrated both the poverty and ignorance of the builders; to the seeing eye, however, it is perfectly clear that so far from being haphazard, the arrangement of these antiquarian *objets trouvés* is as aethestically meaningful as the disposition of the luggage labels and tram tickets in a *collage* by Kurt Schwitters. The interior is quite uninteresting and was heavily restored in the 19th century when the original four columns supporting the dome were replaced by piers. However, the door leading into the *naos* from the narthex has a fine marble surround. Externally the dome is of the regular Athenian type with the silhouette unbroken by projecting eaves over the archivolts, resting on an octagonal drum. Formerly this church was attributed to the 10th century but Mr. Megaw has produced convincing reasons for placing it in the 12th.

The Kapnikaria. The name of this little church, at the bottom of Hermes Street, derives from the title of 'Kapnikaris', the collector of the special tax;

traditionally its foundation is attributed to the Empress Eudoxia, an Athenian by birth, but as it exists today, the structure is largely of the 11th century. It is a cross-in-square of which the angle-chambers may well be later additions, as the *parekklesion* and the multi-gabled exo-narthex certainly are. The three very elegant apses with their windows divided by high columns, a pair in the centre and a singleton in the two side ones, supporting very stilted arches, look to me like a later remodelling, but where all the dates are so keenly disputed by the acknowledged experts I make the point with small conviction.

The Church of the two Theodores. This is an 11th-century church on a modified cross-in-square plan; the dome is supported not on piers or columns but on extensions of the walls separating the angle-chambers from the *naos*. There are three projecting polygonal apses, the central one lit by windows on all three sides. The windows themselves, if not quite so elegant as those in the Kapnikaria, are prettily decorated with cut-brick work and saw-tooth bands. Immediately below the eaves is a pseudo-cufic frieze in terracotta. The walls are made up of largish blocks of rough sandstone, pointed with flat tiles set in the mortaring, a decorative device which became almost standard practice throughout Greece during this period. The bellcote above the gable is certainly a later addition; the Greeks, with their inborn preference for the violently percussive over the possibly melodious, were accustomed to summon the faithful by beating on a wooden plank (symmantron) and the presence of belfries or campaniles is almost always a sign of western influence.

Inside, the church is decorated with wall-paintings by Kantoglou, the Eric Gill of modern Greece. Learned, devout and unashamedly archaising, this extraordinary man is undoubtedly to be numbered among the half-dozen greatest ecclesiastical artists of modern times.

S. Nicodemos. Formerly dedicated to the Panaghia Lycodemou, this church in Odos Phillellonou, not far from its Anglican rival in Early English Gothic, standing on the site of a Roman bath, was in a very ruinous condition when, in the middle of the last century, it was taken over by the Russians. It was then almost completely, but for the date very knowledgeably, rebuilt. Today it is of interest as being not only the largest Byzantine church in the town, but also the only one built on a plan which became increasingly popular in

Greece during the period of the Macedonian Renaissance, of which the most celebrated examples are Daphni, Hosios Loukas and Monemvasia. The central area is covered by a dome on four arches, separated by four squinches in the angles supported on eight piers, a plan which may at first glance appear to western eyes to be complicated and exotic but which is fundamentally the same as that adopted by Wren to build the first dome in England, St. Stephen's Walbrook, the chief difference being that in that splendid church the piers are replaced by pillars and the squinches are surmounted by small angled windows. Here the existence of what amount virtually to aisles, with galleries above, gives to the lay-out an almost basilican slant which is not elsewhere so marked.

With true Slav caution, the church is kept firmly locked between services so that the interior is usually invisible. Apart from keen architectural historians this is likely to be regretted only by devoted amateurs of 19th-century German *bondieuseries* in which it is particularly rich. The campanile, which is entirely modern, possesses a great bell 'remarkably rich and deep in tone' presented by Tsar Alexander II.

S. Soter. Charmingly situated on the north-west flank of the Acropolis overlooking the Plaka, S. Soter, which also appears in some guide books as the church of the Metamorphosis, is a pocket-version of the mini-churches in the town below, the plan of which—three apses, octagonal drum, etc.—it faithfully follows on a minute scale. It was probably erected in the early 14th century, and is the only existing church to have been built in Athens during the Frankish period. Inside it has a grotto chapel cut out of the mountainside and an antique capital serving as the Holy Table.

The Monastery of the Asomatoi. Still on the very outskirts of Athens even as recently as the beginning of the century, the monastery at the top of Patriarch Joachim Street is now hemmed in on all sides by hospitals, embassies and the luxury flats of Kolonaki. Only the apse and east end of the church belong to the original building, west of the *iconostasis* all is 19th century except the monastic buildings round the courtyard which are 20th and surprisingly simple and good. The façade facing the street is painted in stripes of Venetian red and raw siena, a very popular but by no means invariably successful method of decorating churches during the Turkish occupation and after. Nevertheless this curious stylistic mélange is well worth the trouble of search-

The Little Metropolis, Athens

ing out for the sake of the few remaining paintings in the east end which to my mind are the best in Athens.

Omorphi Ekklesia (The Beautiful Church). Quite why this little church, standing on the western slopes of Tourkovouni, should be so distinguished is not at once apparent. A pleasant cross-in-square of the 11th century with the usual dome on an octagonal drum enriched with marble colonettes, a *parekklesion* of slightly later date and a rather scruffy narthex built of rubble, there would appear to be nothing in its construction to render it exceptional, apart from the high quality of the brickwork decoration. If, as seems probable, it owed its name to its situation, it is hardly at present justified, for that part of the plain of Attica which it overlooks, together with the immediately surrounding slopes, today affords an uninterrupted view of what is possibly, with the exception of the Campagna in the immediate neighbourhood of Rome, the most monstrous example of urban expansion in Europe. When I was last there the church was in a very shaky condition but signs of impending restoration were apparent which has now, I believe, taken place. Inside there are some rather faded but interesting wall-paintings, including one of the Ancient of Days, which are said to have been carried out in the 16th century by a painter from Thessaloniki.

Other Athenian churches there are, either so dim or so restored as hardly to be worth seeking out. One or two, however, in the Plaka are pretty enough to pause at, and in Hermes Street is the façade of a pathetic little 11th-century job incorporated, although free-standing, in the ground floor of a vast modern office block, where it looks for all the world like a Christmas display in a department store.

The Byzantine Museum. This well-arranged, but hopelessly overcrowded, museum is housed in the former palace of that extraordinary woman the Duchesse de Plaisance, opposite the British Embassy in Kephissia Street, and should on no account be missed. Particularly good is the collection of church furnishings, including some very beautiful early marble Iconostases.

ATTICA

The Monastery of Kaisariani. For those anxious to follow a contemplative life Mount Hymettus provided a convenient, if suburban, Thebaid; rocky and desolate enough to promote an atmosphere of remoteness it was nonetheless, in Byzantine times, sufficiently well provided with both timber and water to support communal life, and sufficiently far from the city and the sea to afford some security from attack. With the improved conditions of life in the 11th century the original eremitical caves and cabins blossomed into well-appointed monasteries, and numerous churches and chapels were erected on the lower slopes and in the Meszogeion, a flat, fertile plain lying between Hymettus and the mountains around Sunion. Of these the largest and best preserved is the monastery of Kaisariani.

> '*Est prope purpureos colles florentis Hymetti*
> *Fons Sacer . . .*'

This spring which in classical times was sacred to Artemis, to whom a small temple or shrine was dedicated, then provided the main water supply of Athens. Today it continues to bubble away, although no longer emerging from the marble ram's head just inside the monastery wall. Founded in the 11th century the church provides, perhaps, the least altered and most typical example of a Byzantine church interior existing anywhere today. A fully developed cross-in-square in plan, the central dome rests on four pillars with debased Ionic capitals almost certainly taken from the original pagan shrine. The narthex, of which the central bay is surmounted by a dome and cupola, and the *parekklesion* are both later additions, their rubble construction being in strong contrast to the splendid stonework of the church itself in which are incorporated several beautifully carved plaques. But the church's chief distinction lies in its wall-paintings, which are complete, and demonstrate, better than any other series, the iconographic scheme first worked out during the middle Byzantine period. The fact that some are signed and dated as late as 1672 is no indication that the ancient rules were not strictly followed; in the Orthodox Church neither wall-paintings nor icons were ever cleaned; when they became too grubby to be easily comprehended, which, due to the innumerable candles, was very soon, they were repainted by a contemporary who in most cases faithfully followed his predecessor's composition. Here the Pantokrator is in the main dome with a ring of prophets round the drum and the Evangelists in the pendentives; in the apse the Panaghia between archangels surmounts the Divine Liturgy and the Communion of the Apostles; in their duly appointed places are such obligatory scenes as the Baptism, the Anastasis, the Transfiguration, the Incredulity of St. Thomas, the Raising of Lazarus and the Entry into Jerusalem; in the narthex are incidents from the life of the Virgin and, in the dome, the Holy Trinity surrounded by angels and prophets. Elsewhere, on piers and side walls, the customary orthodox saints—Eastern fathers, stylites and warriors—are all present and correct.

On the opposite side of the little courtyard to the church are the refectory and the kitchen, recently thoroughly and thoughtfully restored. During the fearful first winter of the German occupation the pine groves, which had formerly surrounded the monastery, were all cut down, leaving only a few cypresses and two magnificent planes; now, thanks to the energy and enterprise of Madame Argyropoulos, who was also responsible for the restoration, these slopes have all been replanted with the result that Kaisariani is today one of the prettiest spots in Attica.

The Monastery of Asteri. The energetic should know that another, smaller, monastery lies in a little valley higher up the mountain. The church is a cross-in-square with some crumbling wall-paintings, probably of the 16th century, inferior to those in a ruinous refectory alongside. The more easily exhausted may take comfort from the fact that after Kaisariani it is comparatively small beer.

The Monastery of S. John the Theologian. This dilapidated little establishment, of which most of the conventual buildings have long since disappeared, stands in the pylon-dotted, half-developed plain lying between Hymettus and the Kephissia Road. The church, which dates from around 1120, is a cross-in-square with the dome on pillars, but on a slightly simpler plan than that of Kaisariani. Such wall-paintings as remain, chiefly in the apse, are fragmentary and incomplete but of far higher quality, and probably much earlier, than any others on Hymettus. In particular there are some saints' heads, very sensitively painted, of a quite exceptional intensity.

The Monastery of Daoua Penteli. As the name indicates this is situated not on Hymettus but on the slopes of Mount Penteli across the valley, but is not to be confused with the Penteli monastery itself which possesses enormous riches but little interest. Dating from long after the Turkish conquest it is a very odd building indeed. At first glance it appears, with its little corner domes, to bear some resemblance to the original plan of S. Mary Diaconissa in Constantinople, but further investigation proves this to be fortuitous. It has a hexagonal *naos*, as far as I know the only one of its kind, a square apse and an exceptionally lofty narthex crowned with a dome at a considerably higher

level than that over the church itself. Eccentrically conceived and rather incompetently carried out, it cannot be described as an unqualified success.

The Monastery of S. John the Hunter. High on the shoulder of the south-eastern apex of the Hymettan triangle this charming little monastery enjoys one of

the most delightful views in Attica. In the immediate foreground is the descending mountain-side spiked with asphodels; beyond, the great plain of the Mesogeion with its innumerable villages enshrouded in olives and fringed by the bright red soil of the vineyards; in the far distance a strip of ultramarine sea dominated by the mountains of Euboea. The monastery itself, although highly picturesque, is not of any outstanding architectural interest. The usual cross-in-square plan is here masked by the outbuildings which almost completely encircle the church itself, the walls of both being thickly whitewashed. The octagonal drum, however, reveals its brick construction and the windows are nicely treated. The interior, which has been heavily restored, contains little of interest.

The Mesogeion. This district, always the richest in Attica, possesses innumerable churches crowning low hills, tucked away among the vines, or half concealed in the back-streets of towns and villages. Although all are small their plans and elevations differ widely; some are cruciform, some are cross-in-square, some are distinguishable from cow-sheds solely by a projecting apse and a cross on the roof. Domes rest on round or polygonal drums topped by roofs of varying shapes and degrees of flatness; outer walls are whitewashed or striped in Venetian red and raw siena, or, more rarely, are of bare

stone and rubble. There is even, on the road to Porto Raphti, a minute doubled-up basilica with two aisles and two apses.

Many of these churches contain wall-paintings generally late in date, with the usual prescribed scenes in red-bordered panels against a dark blue background, seldom of any great aesthetic importance but frequently charming, many of which are attributed to a painter from Argos named Marko. Both Markopoulo and Koropi, the two principal villages in the area, have several churches apiece in one of which, the church of the Metamorphosis in Koropi, there are recently restored murals said to date from the 10th century. On

top of a hill half a mile south of Liopesi is a rather distinguished, whitewashed church, the dedication of which I have never been able to discover, which contains some distinctly impressive single figures painted with a direct, rather linear technique, in black, ochre and earth-red. In the same neighbourhood is the not dissimilar church of S. Soter, with a dome supported on classical columns taken from some vanished temple.

Despite an admitted absence of architectural masterpieces it can be stated from experience that for the enthusiast few days are likely to prove so enjoyable as one spent church-crawling in the Mesogeion.

The Monastery of Daphni. On the left of the road where the Sacred Motorway from Athens tops the pass before descending to the Bay of Salamis, behind a high castellated wall stands the monastery of Daphni. The octagonal plan,

107

similar to that of the S. Nicodemos in Athens, without the aisles, was first fully developed at Hosios Loukas some sixty years earlier. In order, one suspects, to emphasise the height, which is exceptional, galleries were abandoned, and the dome and squinches are supported on piers unbroken by the horizontal full-stops of capitals that would have been inevitable had pillars been employed. However, it is not to its architecture that Daphni, today, chiefly owes its fame (which is rather unfair, as no Byzantine church is more beautifully proportioned) but to its decoration. The mosaics, of which a surprisingly large number remain in situ, are technically the most competent, as well as the latest in date, of the three great cycles remaining in Greece. Richer than its two rivals, Hosios Loukas and Nea Moni on Chios, Daphni could afford the best, and there is little doubt that these mosaics are the work of artists brought over from, or at least trained in, Constantinople. Refinement and elegance are the qualities that immediately strike one, but after a time one also becomes aware of the delicate flavour of a suave Hellenism of which there is little trace elsewhere in Greece. To those making their first acquaintance with Byzantine art this may well not be apparent, but those familiar with other work of the period may feel, according to their temperament, that there is perhaps almost too much smoothness and elegance, that the self-confidence induced by court-patronage has overlaid intensity. These well-preserved patriarchs, every snow-white curl nicely adjusted, and superbly robed angels with not a feather out of place, undoubtedly make their megalocephalic counterparts at Hosios Loukas look gauche by comparison, but the latter display a sturdiness and strength of religious purpose which is not very noticeable here and which some will miss. The Crucifixion, for instance, moving and beautifully composed as it is, is far closer in feeling to Perugino than to Giotto. However, it should always be borne in mind that these mosaics have been heavily and frequently restored, and that at a time when restorers did not hesitate to make little personal readjustments to obtain a closer conformity to contemporary ideals. There is, however, one mosaic in the presence of which no reservations are possible—the great Pantokrator in the dome.

There is here no trace of Hellenism; the conception is wholly Eastern and as far removed from the Good Shepherd at Ravenna as from the Light of the World. Of all the Pantokrators in the Byzantine lands, from Kiev to Cefalu, this is the most awe-inspiring and convincing.[1]

[1] If, as seems unlikely but some maintain, it is largely the work of an Italian restorer in the last century, the man was a genius of a very rare order.

Most of the marble revetments which formerly covered the lower walls have long since vanished and large areas, which were up to a very few years ago unadorned stonework, have latterly been covered with a particularly unattractive mud-coloured cement. Compared to S. Vitale or SS. Sergius and Bacchus there is little carved stonework remaining, but the string courses, particularly that round the base of the dome, are quite exceptionally delicate and splendid. The exo-narthex is supported on pointed arches which date, as does the gallery above, from the period of the Frankish Duchy of Athens when the Cistercians liberated the monastery from the Schismatics.

Externally the church has a very noble and dignified appearance. The enthusiasm for rich and elaborate wall decoration, which characterised those churches built at the beginning of the 11th century, had by now spent itself and here a comparatively simple key-pattern, carried out in tiles, replaces the pseudo-cufic friezes, and there are no inset plaques or other cloisonné effects. The walls are constructed of beautifully hewn stone blocks, occasionally set in the shape of a cross, divided by arrangements of flat tiles. Such decoration as exists is confined almost entirely to the window surrounds and is carried out in brick.

BOEOTIA

On leaving Daphni, the old road to the north, after skirting Eleusis, climbs a couple of low passes and crosses into Boeotia beneath the walls of the great fortress of Eleftheria. All along the way are small anonymous chapels set on low hills, none perhaps worth an expedition for its own sake but all agreeable picnic rendezvous. Just before the road starts its final climb out of Attica

there is a turning on the left leading down to Aegosthena on the Gulf of Corinth. Those who set out to visit this celebrated classical site should not miss the opportunity of taking a look at the tiny whitewashed Byzantine church, dedication unknown, which stands on an adjacent slope. Of late but

indeterminate date, a modest cruciform in plan, it is beautifully typical rather than in any way remarkable. Inside, in addition to the usual fly-blown oleographs and the smell of beeswax candles, are a few faded paintings of no exceptional merit but including, on the north wall, a very charming S. George complete with coffee-boy that seems to be the work of a rather more competent artist than whoever was responsible for the remainder.

The Panaghia of Skripou. Off to the right of the main road after leaving Thebes, rising above the drained fields of Lake Copais, is the site of 'Golden Orchomenos'. Just below it stands the remarkable church of the Dormition of Our Lady of Skripou. Firmly dated, for once, 873, this is possibly the oldest existing church in Greece, certainly the oldest cruciform. Its plan is of particular interest as marking the first stage in the development of the familiar cross-in-square from the basilica with transepts. Over an exceptionally high crossing, a dome is supported on four barrel vaults covering the *naos*, *bema* and the two transepts; on the north and west are aisles, also barrel-vaulted, but on a much lower level, terminating in semi-circular apses; on the west is a narthex covered with a transverse barrel vault. The aisles are continuous, piercing the transepts as in any Romanesque church but, simply by enclosing them on the east and west, the plan is immediately transformed into a cross-in-square.

Some have detected in this church the influence of contemporary Bulgarian building, which is possible, and in the carved decoration, within and without, Sassanian inspiration, which seems to me less likely. Although not perhaps outstandingly beautiful, the church undoubtedly possesses a massive and formidable dignity and notably splendid proportions.

PHOCIS

The Monastery of Hosios Loukas. The road from Livadia to Delphi climbs steadily up to the summit of a pass where stands the village of Arachova. Some few miles on the near side of this a turning goes off to the left leading to the tragic village of Distomo whence another, replacing the mule-track of twenty years ago, goes on to the Monastery of the Blessed Luke. The career of this pious and unfortunate man should entitle him, if ever he finally achieves canonisation, to be regarded as the patron saint of Displaced Persons. Born on Aegina, he was forced to flee the island owing to the depredations of Arab corsairs and take refuge in Kastoria. Shortly afterwards the Bulgarians descended from the north and he and his family took flight to the Gulf of Corinth which was immediately laid waste by the Hungarians. After this last experience he decided to abandon the world and establish himself in this safely remote valley where the fame of his piety soon attracted numerous disciples. Great as this may have been, it would hardly have kept his name alive today had it not been accompanied by a gift of prophecy which, at least on one occasion, was spectacularly exercised when he foretold the recapture of Crete from the Arabs by an Emperor called Romanus. When some twenty years after his death this prophecy was duly fulfilled, the wife of the Emperor (Romanus II), Theophano, the mother of the Bulgar-Slayer, straightway decided to honour the prophet's memory by the erection of a splendid shrine over his last resting place, and artists and architects were at once sent out from the capital. Unfortunately work languished as, after the death of Romanus, his wife married a gloomy general, Nicephorus Phocas, who was the reverse of open-handed and not at all interested in commemorating the triumphs of his predecessor, and it was not until he, too, had been eliminated by Theophano, and succeeded by her son, that work was resumed.

In the 17th century the monastery was visited by the Reverend Sir George Wheler, some time Rector of Houghton, who declared it to be the finest church in all Greece after Hagia Sophia 'notwithstanding it is very old and hath suffered much by earthquake and time'. Today it is three centuries older and in addition to earthquake has suffered from the Turks in the 19th century and the Germans in the 20th, but nevertheless the Reverend Wheler's claim can still be maintained. The credit must go, in part, to those responsible for the recent restoration; in 1945 the floors were ankle-deep in fallen tesserae, the piers were shaky from bombing, great holes gaped in the roof. Now the mosaics are safely replaced, the very beautiful revetments once more complete and the structure sound. All one can justifiably regret is the presence of the hard, red, modern tiles on the dome and roofs.

The monastery contains two adjacent churches, the *katholikon*, which is the larger and was built around 1020, that is to say just after Basil II's visit to Greece, while the smaller, the Theotokos, is some thirty years later. The plan of the *katholikon* is fundamentally the same as that of Daphni, which derives from it, but, owing to the galleries and the screens of columns across the transepts, appears at first glance more complicated. Externally only the central apse projects and the cross-vaulted transepts do not extend beyond the side walls; there are windows on two levels which, together with some elaborate decoration in stone and brick, produce an unusually rich effect.

Within, not only are the mosaics more numerous and complete than those at Daphni, but all the marble veneer which sheathes the piers and the lower part of the walls is intact, as is the very beautiful floor of *opus Alexandrinum*.

The great series of mosaics must be regarded as a whole; examined individually, many are stiff, some are unimaginative and one or two singularly ill-drawn, but the total effect is overwhelming. Hosios Loukas was always remote and its monks enjoyed a reputation for austerity which is often reflected in the treatment of single figures; in particular the military saints are a far tougher looking bunch than their fellows at Daphni.

The arrangement and disposition of the various scenes follows more closely than in any other church the strict scheme evolved in the post-iconoclastic period; Old and New Testament incidents are carefully balanced and even the use of colour conforms exactly to the established system. Of the several artists employed the majority were probably provincials, although Prof. Demus claims that one possibly hailed from Constantinople, and in their work display marked differences, both of style and accomplishment. The finest, to my mind, are the saints and angels in roundels in the angles of many of the cross-vaults in the side chapels and transepts; the most gauche, some of the Fathers with out-sized heads in the exo-narthex. The Pantokrator has vanished from the main dome, as has the Annunciation from one of the supporting squinches, but there is a most beautiful head and shoulders of Christ over the main door of the narthex.

After the *katholikon* the Theotokos may well strike the visitor as bare and rather dull, relying as it does solely on its proportions for its effect. A straightforward cross-in-square closely enclosed by the side walls, the dome is supported on classical columns. Some critics profess to find the elaborate carving of the capitals and the string-courses stiff and formal, but they seem to me admirably to fulfil their aesthetic function. The marble iconostasis is a masterpiece comparable in the quality of its workmanship to that at Torcello, and there is another splendid pavement. Externally the principal feature of the church is the very elegant little cupola over the dome with its intricately carved stone panels in which some have detected signs of Islamic influence.

Outside the two churches on a wide terrace is a small, but comfortable, guest-house where the keen sightseer is unreservedly recommended to stay. After the last coachload of tourists has gone and the souvenir stall has closed its shutters, the terrace reverts to the status of a small *platia*; the peasants come up from the villages in the valley below and, having taken their children to kiss the icons, stop for a gossip with the monks; the last of the sun slides off the highest mountain-top to the east, and before one has finished a second ouzo the moon is suddenly and dramatically up. And then in the morning one has the churches for two hours to oneself before the first bus from Delphi comes hooting up the road below.

GALAXIDION

From Delphi the road drops down into the Vale of Amphissa and goes on to Itea where, as a practical proposition, it comes to an end. However, beyond the lignite mines to the west a lorry track continues round the edge of the Gulf to the small town of Galaxidion. Here are two churches, the Paraskevi and S. Nikolaos, both comparatively modern and neither of outstanding interest, but the latter containing one of the largest and most intricately carved of all those wooden screens which became so popular in the 18th and 19th centuries. The craftsman who was responsible, Baba Nicolas of Epirus, was so pleased with his handiwork that he deliberately made it several sizes too large, thus gaining the satisfaction of having the existing church largely rebuilt in order to accommodate his masterpiece. If this is the sort of thing you like, you will like it very much.

A couple of miles to the west of the town up a steep mule track winding through the olive groves is the Monastery of the Saviour built by Manuel II, Despot of Epirus, to celebrate his deliverance from the wiles of a sorceress known as the Lady Gangrene. A simple hall-church, to which a transverse gable lends an illusion of being cruciform, it is of no great architectural interest but highly picturesque. Inside there are some faded wall-paintings and on the outside, at the east end, is a carved plaque which, so far as one can judge through layers of whitewash, would seem to be of high quality.

Even if the buildings are judged small reward for a stiff climb, the view from the terrace across the Gulf of Itea to Delphi, with the great mass of Parnassos above and beyond, is one of the most spectacular in Greece.

EPIRUS

By an appalling road inland from Galaxidion it is possible, with luck and perseverance, to cross the wild uplands of Aetolia and come down on the walled port of Navpaktos, opposite Patras, whence a rather better road, skirting the tepid waters of the Ambracian Gulf, leads eventually to Arta, the principal town of Southern Epirus.

After the Latin Conquest, Epirus maintained its independence under a Despot, Manuel II, a bastard cousin of the Imperial House then reigning in exile in Nicaea, who treated on equal terms with the various Latin principalities and with the Venetians. During this period Arta flourished and close relations were maintained with the West, particularly with the Angevins in Naples, and most of the principal monuments in the town were built.

The Panaghia Paragoritissa (Our Lady the All-Compassionate). This large church is perhaps the most extraordinary in the whole Empire, and from the outside the least attractive. Seen from the west it resembles nothing so much as an old-fashioned biscuit-box crowned with five symmetrically disposed pepper-pots and a filigree salt-cellar. Uncompromisingly square, the external walls are broken by two rows of rather clumsy round-headed windows, enlivened here and there by bits of chequer-work, and on the east by three large apses. The inside, although not quite so depressingly unimaginative, is far, far odder. The central area conforms, very eccentrically, to the middle Byzantine octagonal plan; the dome is supported on four arches with four very reduced squinches in the angles, but the arches themselves are carried, not on piers or pillars, but on three superimposed orders of columns, their bases resting on consoles corbelled out from the walls. Surrounding the *naos* on three sides are rather high aisles surmounted by lofty galleries, and what would, elsewhere, be the transepts are cut off by solid walls and, together with the *prothesis* and the *diakonikon*, form what are virtually separate side chapels. Around the north and south arches are bands of carved beasts and saints and some of the corbels are, rather hamfistedly, sculpted in animal forms.

While Western influence is undoubted, the curious thing about this decoration is that it is Romanesque in character rather than Gothic (of which signs are visible in the tracery of one of the squinches), for at the end of the 13th

115

century, when the church was built, Romanesque had to all intents and purposes vanished from Western Europe and had never flourished in the Neapolitan area with which Epirote connections were closest. In the central dome are remains of mosaics, a fine Pantokrator surrounded by prophets and angels, which are not easy to study without field-glasses.

Twenty years ago the condition of the church was appalling. The structure was badly shaken by bombing, the dome was severely cracked, and the faded and not very interesting wall-paintings were almost obliterated by the droppings of a large colony of rooks which inhabited the galleries. Now, I gather, the necessary repairs have been duly carried out and the church has been opened as a museum.

There are two other churches in Arta, S. Theodora and S. Basil. The former was traditionally built by S. Theodora herself, the wife of the Despot who became entangled with the Lady Gangrene, but probably incorporates an earlier foundation. Basilical in plan, with a narthex and exo-narthex, there are ancient columns with fine capitals in the *naos* and some traces of painting. In the narthex is the shrine of the saint, on the outside of which she is depicted, crowned and robed, together with her son, in low relief. The paired columns, secured by loops which enclose the panel, together with the rather naïf treatment of the figures, suggest a strong Romanesque influence. The church of S. Basil, which dates from the 14th century, is decorated externally with both ornamental brickwork and glazed tiles; in addition on the east wall are two glazed, polychromatic, panels, one of the Crucifixion, the other of the Three Hierarchs. The barn-like interior, wooden-roofed, can safely be missed. Across the river is the small monastic church of Vlachernae, a cruciform basilica probably dating from the 13th century, which is said to contain the remnants of a very beautiful marble screen of Constantinopolitan workmanship.

THE PELOPONNESE

During the centuries after the collapse of Roman power the Peloponnese, or Morea, suffered as much as, if not more than, the rest of Greece. The isthmus of Corinth proved no obstacle in the way of Barbarian incursions and large bands of Slavs roamed the area at will. The prosperity of such great commercial cities as Corinth withered away almost overnight and large areas in the centre and south relapsed into a barbarism from which they had only partially ever emerged. It is not surprising, therefore, that, apart from the foundations of the basilica at Corinth and the church at Olympia, there are virtually no traces of Byzantine architecture pre-dating the Macedonian renaissance. Of 11th- and 12th-century buildings there are, however, many splendid examples, mostly in the neighbourhood of Argos, in which the characteristic brick ornamentation of the period achieves, perhaps, its finest development.

After the Latin Conquest, most of the area passed into the hands of the Villehardouin family who styled themselves Princes of Achaea and controlled their fiefs from their great castle at Mistra on the slopes of Mount Taygetus overlooking Sparta. However, the greatest of these Norman princelings, William de Villehardouin, overplayed his hand and, embarking on an expedition against the Byzantine possessions on the mainland, was soundly defeated and forced to hand over three of his principal strongholds, including Mistra, to the Greeks. From now until the middle of the 15th century when it was surrendered to the Turks, Mistra, under the rule of the semi-independent Despots of the Morea, who were usually connections of the Imperial House, flourished more spectacularly than any city in the Empire. The great Norman keep and walls were reinforced; a palace built; and innumerable churches and monasteries established of which a large number miraculously remain. The paintings with which many of these last are decorated provided, until the uncovering of those in the Kahriye Djami, the principal evidence on which our knowledge of the Palaeologan revival of the arts was based. If none of them quite attain to the grandeur of the great Anastasis in the Capital, they include several splendid works, and as a series their value is aesthetic as well as historical. Moreover, here, better than almost anywhere else, one can follow the development of two schools in late Byzantine painting, the Macedonian and the Cretan. The former is characterised by free and rather dashing brushwork, a fondness for large, open forms and a marked tendency towards generalisation; the latter, more linear in style and more intense in colour, relates more closely to the work of the icon-painters.

The aftermath of the Turkish Conquest was a great deal more agitated in the Morea than elsewhere in Greece. The highland clans of the Mani were never successfully subdued; there were Albanian revolts, and the Venetians were for long active and successful. They recaptured Mistra in the 17th century, only to lose it again in the 18th and retained their hold on Monemvasia until 1715, and towards the end of the period there was even an abortive Russian expedition under the command of the celebrated Orloff. That little

or no church-building was undertaken in these troubled circumstances is hardly a matter for surprise.

MERBAKA

This tiny village, lying a mile or two to the east of the Argos–Nauplion road in the neighbourhood of Tiryns, takes its name from a Dutchman, William de Meerbeeke, who was bishop here during the Latin Conquest. Today it consists of three or four cottages and a magnificent church. This last is, perhaps, the finest existing example anywhere of the fully developed cross-in-square plan; the nobly proportioned dome rises on an octagonal drum adorned with pilasters at the angles; there are three polygonal apses; the north–south arms of the cross which rise above, but do not project beyond, the exterior walls are adorned by three-light windows flanked by high-shouldered blank brick quadrants, a typically Greek procedure; and the whole building rests on a marble podium. The interior is of little interest apart from richly carved Corinthian capitals to the pillars topped with im-post-blocks, but the exquisite decoration of the outside provides abundant compensation. Above the line of a moulded string course, crowning the base of marble blocks, the masonry is of beautifully dressed stone divided by courses of tiles and is enriched by every decorative device known to the builders of the middle Byzantine period—herringbone brickwork, dogtooth bands, meanders of carefully arranged tiles and a variety of inset *objets trouvés* ranging from ceramic plates to a Byzantine sundial—but disposed with a discretion and a restraint not always achieved in earlier years. Built in the late 12th century, it was restored and enlarged after the Latin Conquest when the existing narthex and bellcote were added.

Hagia Moni. On the right of the road from Nauplion to Epidauros stands the monastery of Hagia Moni (called in some guide-books by the name of the village, Areia) which is dated 1149 and is possibly a slightly earlier work by the architect of Merbaka. The plan is almost identical and all the same decorative devices are employed with an equal tact. The general effect is slightly less massive and there are minor differences—four sides of the octagonal drum have blank arcades and the windows of the transepts have single lights. It has also retained its porch and exo-narthex, both of which have disappeared at Merbaka. Like the latter it was added to at a later date and there are signs of Western influences, i.e. the bellcote and some curious cusping around the window of the central apse.

The interior contains what the local guide-book describes as 'peintures exceptionelles', possibly rightly, because for sheer unrelieved 19th-century horror they are quite unrivalled. Formerly the little garden surrounding the church was perhaps the prettiest monastic garden in Greece, but on my last

visit much of the charm had been successfully dissipated by the erection of some monstrous modernistic cloisters in concrete.

There are two other churches belonging to this group in the immediate neighbourhood, one at Chonika, between Argos and the Hieraion, and the other, smaller and ruinous, at Plataniti. Neither, however, is in quite the same class of accomplishment as Merbaka and Hagia Moni. There is also a small chapel in the cemetery on the Tripolis road which looks to me from a distance, for I have never been able to get in, of the same type, but maybe is a modern rebuilding.

LIGOURION

Halfway between Nauplion and Epidauros lies the village of Ligourion, outside which is a small but interesting church dedicated to S. Joannis. Built about 1080, it is rather earlier than the previous group and the external decoration is far less elaborate. Cross-in-square in plan, the central area is vaulted at a proportionately greater height than usual, and traces of the wooden centering are still visible in the dome, at least to the eye of faith. Externally only the central apse projects and there is a small narthex. The line of the eaves above the octagonal drum is straight, as at Merbaka, but it has been suggested that originally it followed the curves of the arcading framing the windows, producing that wavy effect common in Attica, and was remodelled at some later date.

The interior is shabby, with a few faint traces of blackened wall-paintings, but does not lack atmosphere. Seen from without, this rather battered and slightly top-heavy little church, facing the village fountain and backed by almond trees, produces a very agreeable effect.

MISTRA

This extraordinary dead city, set on a steep, sunbaked mountainside with its vertiginous, crumbling walls, its ruined cisterns and foundations treacherously masked by thyme and Jerusalem sage, and its quantity of churches, is today principally celebrated for its wall-paintings. These are numerous, frequently fine, and have given rise to more controversy than perhaps any other group of frescoes in the world. The dates, the artists and, above all, the merits of these works have been, and continue to be, matters for the liveliest dispute; Byron and Talbot-Rice, Diehl and Millet, Muratoff and Grabar, all support different theories and roundly condemn each other's conclusions. At Mistra the conscientious art-lover is not just advised but compelled to use his own judgement.

SS. Theodoroi. This, the earliest of the Mistra churches, despite the fact that it was built around 1290, that is to say under the Palaeologues, conforms closely both in layout and decoration to the churches of the preceding period. The octagonal plan is similar to that of Daphni and the exterior is enriched with herringbone brickwork, dog-tooth bands and high-shouldered windows, as at Merbaka, and the lancets in the drum, which is dodecagonal, are separated by blank niches as at Hagia Moni. The church, which has recently been repaired, was roofless for many years and the remaining paintings, which include a portrait of Manuel Palaeologos kneeling before Our Lord, have suffered in consequence. In the pavement a double-headed eagle commemorates the coronation of the last Byzantine Emperor.

The Metropolis or S. Demetrios. The present church, which was built early in the 14th century by Archbishop Nicephoros Moschopoulos, replaced an earlier basilical structure, some fragments of which it incorporates. The better and earlier of the two groups of paintings are those in the *bema*; dignified and hieratic, they are, despite their comparatively late date, quite uninfluenced by the humanistic tendencies of the Palaeologan revival and might well have been painted a hundred or more years earlier. Particularly impressive is the Virgin in the apse, statuesque and remote, recalling Torcello. In the dome is a fine Hetoimasia with angels, perhaps the latest example of a theme very popular in the early period of Byzantine art. The remaining paintings in the *naos* and narthex, scenes from the Life of Christ and the Martyrdom of St. Demetrios, are later in date and probably the work of an artist of the Macedonian school.

The whole cycle of paintings in this church are generally dismissed as stiff and uninteresting, notably by Byron and Talbot-Rice, but are considered by Muratoff to be the finest in Mistra.

The Brontocheion or Aphendiko. The Brontocheion was the richest and most important monastery in the Morea and this church, built a year or two later than the Metropolis, was suitably impressive and perhaps the last ever to be enriched with marble revetment (now vanished). The plan is of the greatest interest; basilical at ground-level and cruciform above, it recalls that of S. Irene at Constantinople, with the addition of domes over the angle-chambers, and may be regarded as a classic example of that tendency

towards revivalism that recurred from time to time throughout Byzantine history. To my mind the interior is architecturally the finest of any church in Mistra, the arcades cutting off the transepts from the *naos* are beautifully proportioned and exactly related to the galleries above, and one here has the feeling, only induced by first-rate buildings, that the problem of space has been fully understood and brilliantly solved.

The paintings are fragmentary and not too well preserved and, while individually they do not compare with the finest of the single scenes in the Peribleptos and the Pantanassa, I have the impression that, when complete, the whole cycle was probably rather more satisfactory in relationship to the architecture. The most impressive of those that remain are the head of the priest Zacharias in one of the domes and a remarkable composition in a small side chamber in which *chrysobuls*, or imperial edicts, are unrolled by angels. Today the church is no longer in the appalling condition which justifiably excited the righteous indignation of Robert Byron; admirably restored, the hideous new tiles are the only feature likely to arouse criticism.

The Evangelistra. This church, not far from the Metropolis, is probably a funerary chapel dating from the early 14th century. Cross-in-square in plan, it is built of dressed stones pointed with tiles, has three projecting apses and an octagonal drum on which the line of the eaves is broken by the projecting archivolts of the four windows that alternate with niches. Externally it produces a rather muddled effect owing both to the site and to additional buildings, and the interior is of no great interest.

Hagia Sophia. Built in 1350 by Manuel Cantacuzenos, immediately above the Palace of the Despots, this was the court church. Its plan resembles that of the Evangelistra and the exterior is similarly cluttered up with ossuaries and *parekklesions*. Formerly it was in a semi-ruinous condition and only traces of wall-paintings appear to have survived, but it has recently been restored and more paintings, reportedly of some merit, have been discovered under coats of whitewash in a side-chapel.

The Peribleptos. Basically, the church, which probably dates from the middle of the 14th century, is a cross-in-square with a prolonged western arm and no narthex, but the plan is complicated by an additional chamber to the north, an irregular *parekklesion* on the west, and the fact that it is partially cut out of the hillside. On the main apse is a fleur-de-lis between rosettes which, together with a trefoil on an adjacent tower and the prolongation of the nave, suggest Western influence.

On first entering, the interior seems dark, mysterious and predominantly blue, and it is some moments before one becomes fully aware of the wealth of painting that surrounds one. According to Millet there were two artists engaged, one conforming to the Cretan tradition, whose work displays extraordinary delicacy and finish, the other employing a looser, more impressionistic technique and possibly influenced by the Macedonian school.

124

Hagia Sophia, Monemvasia

The former's masterpiece is the Divine Liturgy in the main apse where Our Lord, robed as a priest, celebrates beneath a *ciborium*, flanked by a procession of angels with blue and green wings clad in long white surplices; the painting of these last, and the suggestion of the form and movement underneath them, is a technical feat of the highest order, and the whole scene must rank amongst the finest achievements of Byzantine painting. Hardly less impressive are the Transfiguration in the adjacent aisle, with its intense figure of Christ surrounded by a great mandorla and the scene of the two Marys at the Empty Tomb, in which the pose and placing of the angel are almost exactly paralleled in a picture of the same subject by Duccio in Siena, painted nearly a century earlier. (Any direct influence need not, however, be assumed; probably both artists were working from illuminated manuscripts deriving from the same original source.)

Of the other group the most striking, to my mind, is the Entry into Jerusalem, dominated by the figure in the foreground wearing a boldly striped cloak.

The Monastery of the Pantanassa. The earlier 15th-century church of this little monastery, which still shelters a handful of nuns, is architecturally the most interesting, if not the most beautiful, of all the Mistra churches. Terraced on a steeply sloping hillside, it is not properly orientated; the axis is closer to north–south than to east–west, and it is equipped with a loggia, similar perhaps to that which once existed alongside the Brontocheion and with a campanile of a decidedly Western character. Externally the three apses are decorated with two bands of blind arcading, the upper of the normal round-headed Byzantine type, the lower of narrow lancets topped by pointed arches, which are separated by a border of strap-work loops, slightly out of proportion to the rest of the ornamentation, terminating in flower-like finials. The overall effect is rather that of some neo-Gothic folly or toll-house conceived by Batty Langley.

The plan is of the same revivalist type as that of the Brontocheion with galleries and narthex (the exo-narthex has vanished). Of the domes only the largest, and that over the central bay of the narthex, project externally, the remainder being covered by a continuous roof, a sure sign of Western influence.

The numerous paintings still adorning the interior are regarded by some as the finest flowering of the Palaeologan revival, foreshadowing the Italian Renaissance; others prefer the quieter colouring and less demonstrative quality of those in the Peribleptos. What, however, in both series is most likely to strike the visitor who is not a *kunstforscher*, is not so much signs of a new humanistic approach, as the fidelity with which the old, prescribed, formulae are still adhered to. In the Nativity, the Virgin lies diagonally in the usual rocky cleft, with the two attendants preparing to wash the Babe in the foreground, the Magi popping up from behind the cardboard mountains on the left, and the angels, shepherds and cattle all in their accustomed places as they are at Hosios Loukas, Daphni and in innumerable manuscripts; in the Entry into Jerusalem the same figure in the same striped cloak dominates the foreground and the Presentation in the Temple takes place against those same strangely curved architectural elements which occur both in S. Mark's and the Kahriye Djami. Such extreme conformity might well have produced an inhibiting effect (as it undoubtedly did in Ancient Egypt), but the Byzantine experience successfully demonstrates that for the first-rate artist who is not a genius it may well prove a source of strength; freed from any obsessive urge to be original at all costs, he can concentrate on intensifying the internal significance of the scene by his handling of paint and colour, and by inconspicuous personal re-adjustments within the accepted and clearly defined compositional framework provided and enforced by ecclesiastical tradition.

Monemvasia

Far down on the easternmost prong of the Peloponnese there rises, just offshore, but joined to the mainland by a causeway, the great rock of Monemvasia. Heavily fortified from an early period, it was captured from the Greeks by William de Villehardouin in 1249 after a prolonged siege, but less than twenty years later was returned by treaty at the same time as Mistra. In 1464 it fell to the Venetians, in 1540 to the Turks, back to the Venetians in 1690, and finally to the Turks in 1715. With this history, it is hardly surprising that the architectural tradition is not distinguished by continuity.

In the lower town are four churches of which the identification is not rendered any easier by the fact that no two guide-books, and few of the inhabitants, agree on the dedications. Of these, three are of the same type, all late in date, one having been built during the final Venetian occupation, and showing strong traces of Western influence. The circumference of the drum is rather larger than that of the dome, which itself rests on pointed arches and is left unroofed and faced with cement, as are the barrel vaults over the arms of the cross (churches of an exactly similar kind occur frequently in Cyprus at the same date). The largest of these may safely be identified as the Metropolis, thanks to the presence over the west door of a Byzantine slab decorated with peacocks which was mentioned by Colonel Leake.[1] Inside, the iconostasis is adorned with some very late icons, heavily, and to me unfortunately, influenced by the Venetian Renaissance. The fourth church in the lower town, although probably of even later date, has a more familiar aspect. It is cross-in-square in plan and decorated externally in stripes of yellow, white and blue; within is to be found a miraculous icon, the handiwork, so it is said, of St. Luke himself, which was drawn up from the sea in a bucket and still

commands the veneration of the few remaining inhabitants of this picturesque but melancholy stronghold.

On the very summit of the rock, surrounded by ruinous curtain-walls and fortified gates, rises the great Church of Hagia Sophia, most spectacularly situated of all Byzantine places of worship, built by Andronicus the Second in the late 13th century. For its date both the plan and decoration are old-fashioned, akin to Daphni and Hosios Loukas; the drum is polygonal, the dome rests on an octagon and the transepts have three-light windows. The most unusual feature is the row of short, flat-topped openings enriched with Renaissance mouldings, now blocked-up, which once connected the galleries with a much later narthex, an insertion dating from Venetian times. There are also some good carved stonework and the remains of wall-paintings, also rather old-fashioned, mostly of martyrs. Exhausted as the visitor may be by

[1] *Travels in the Morea*, John Murray, 1830.

the climb, he should on no account fail to go round to the north side of the church, where a small terrace crowns a great cliff with a sheer drop of 800 ft. to the ultramarine below.

THE WEST COAST

Outside the three great architectural centres, of the Argolid, Mistra and Monemvasia, there exist many isolated churches, particularly in the Mani and at Yeraki, south of Sparta, but only a few of these are both interesting and readily accessible to the ordinary traveller.

GASTOUNI

This small and unimportant village, the name of which is a corruption of the Frankish 'Gastogne', as it is still referred to in some older guide-books, is situated on the flat coastal plain just off the main road from Olympia to Patras. A small but very beautiful cross-in-square, dating, I imagine, from the early 12th century, it has an octagonal drum, triple windows in the transepts, dog-toothed bands, meanders and even an inset classical inscription. On the north wall is an ogival arch dating from the time when the church was being used by the Franks for their own rites.

It shelters another of St. Luke's strangely numerous icons, the exact provenance of which is explained in strip-cartoon form on a painted banner in the *bema*. It was, apparently, found up a palm tree by a pious Ethiopian who was whisked through the air, together with the tree and the icon, and finally dropped on an easily recognisable Gastouni. As the icon itself is almost entirely covered with silver plates, confirmation of this attribution on stylistic grounds is not easy.

MANOULADA

Further along the same road, between Andravida and Patras, half hidden by reeds, lies the picturesque and highly curious little church of Manoulada. The plan, most unusual in these parts, is straight cruciform, lacking the usual angle chambers; the dome, resting on a high octagonal drum, is naked and untiled externally, and there is a single polygonal apse and a complete absence of tile-courses. When last I saw it, the condition was bad and the exterior adorned with a crop of weeds and grasses which the locals, feeling that the Virgin, to whom the church is dedicated, might prefer it that way, refused to remove. Now, I assume, and hope, it is in much better shape.

OLYMPIA

The Olympic Games were finally suppressed by the Emperor Theodosius in A.D. 393. The triumph of Christianity was shortly afterwards commemorated by the foundation of a church, close to what was left of the Theocleion (house of the soothsayers), on a site which may possibly have been that of Phidias' studio in which he produced the model for the celebrated chryselephantine statue of Zeus. Basilical in plan, with a single apse, the lower courses of the wall, which may perhaps have been those of the earlier building, are of stone, the upper of brick. There remains an ambo, with two flights of steps, a pierced marble screen and, in the nave, fragments of some curious Ionic columns, oval in section and elaborately fluted. The over-elaboration of the ornament and the lack of imagination with which it is applied provide depressing evidence of how run down proto-Byzantine decoration had become in the 5th century.

6

THE AEGEAN AND CRETE

D URING most of the Byzantine period the Greek Archipelago seldom enjoyed any long period of tranquillity. Although less exposed to barbarian inroads, most of the islands suffered far more regularly than the mainland from the activities of pirates and sea-raiders, particularly after the arrival in the Mediterranean of the Arabs, with the result that the inhabitants frequently abandoned the old classical towns on the seashore and built themselves far less commodious, but generally rather safer, retreats inland, usually on the most easily defensible of the local peaks. Seaborne trade, on which most of the islands depended, declined, and only a handful possessed any alternative source of income. Corn was still grown on Thasos, marble still quarried at Paros and iron mined on Serifos, but for the rest, few could support more than a small population of fisherfolk and some were totally abandoned. However, the Latin Conquest, the effects of which were elsewhere so disastrous, had certain advantages for the Archipelago. Many of the islands passed into the hands of the Franks, and remained in them long after the liberation of Byzantium itself, and the new rulers, particularly the Venetians, were usually rather better equipped than the old central government to maintain order and protect communications. They were, however, Roman Catholics, and if the local Orthodox were seldom subjected to persecution as they were on Cyprus, they were exposed to some pressure, reinforced by the promise of various concessions, both economic and social, to embrace the Roman faith. That large numbers succumbed is proved by the fact that today the majority of Greek Catholics are to be found in the islands.

With such a history it is hardly surprising that the Aegean, apart from Crete, has few examples of Byzantine architecture that can compare with the more remarkable of those on the mainland. Such churches as may have existed during the earliest Christian period would have been in the abandoned sea-ports and either destroyed by the Arabs or used as building material for the new strongholds on the mountain-tops; those erected later under foreign domination were small and discreet. From the two great periods of Byzantine building there remain only the Church of the Virgin on Paros and that of the Monastery of Nea Moni on Chios.

Nevertheless, almost every island possesses a few churches and chapels, invariably small, perched on headlands or crowning hilltops, which, although seldom of great architectural importance, are usually well worth the stroll. The majority, particularly in the Cyclades, conform to an established norm; barrel-vaulted and untiled, the usually rather irregular exterior, including the dome, is thickly covered with whitewash, so that one has the impression that the whole building has been cut out of a block of fibre-glass by hand. Sometimes the dome is painted Reckitt's blue, and where Italian influence has been strong there are often arcaded bellcotes.

To catalogue these humble shrines would be the work of a lifetime, and in the following chapter I have confined myself to indicating the whereabouts of such as are known to me, and to the description of those which are of acknowledged interest.

THE CYCLADES

PAROS

The Panaghia Hecatonpyliani, Our Lady of the Hundred Gates, is the finest and, with the possible exception of Gortyna on Crete, the oldest church in the islands. Standing a little outside the town, it traditionally marks the spot where St. Helena had the dream which led to her discovery of the Cross. She herself left instructions in her will for the erection of a church, but two hundred years would seem to have elapsed before they were carried out, and the present buildings, which date from the mid-6th century, were commissioned by Justinian, who is said to have employed an architect who had worked on Hagia Sophia.

The plan is complicated by the fact that it includes three buildings under the same roof. The main church is a domed basilica with aisles, galleries and transepts with, enclosed in the north-east angle of the cross, the smaller, slightly earlier, church of S. Nikolaos, likewise galleried and aisled but lacking transepts. On the south side is a baptistry that contains one of those curious cruciform sitz-bath fonts so common in North Africa in early Christian times. In the main apse there is a *synthronon* and an altar beneath a *ciborium*;

both churches have fine stone screens, and in the smaller is the wooden shrine of St. Theoctiste of Lesbos, who lived for many years as an anchoress in the church during the period when it was deserted. A curious feature is that while the aisles are arcaded, with Ionic pillars topped by impost-blocks, in the galleries square piers, separated by carved stone panels, support an entablature. If 'gates' is interpreted in the widest sense as including arcade openings and screens, it is just possible that this singularly beautiful church justifies its name, but no one, so far as I know, has ever checked. The main building was extensively repaired in the 17th and 18th centuries when the nave was re-roofed, and the last time I was there it was undergoing a further very thorough, and apparently careful, restoration which should by now be complete.

Elsewhere in the town are several small churches, whitewashed and half smothered in bougainvillea and Morning Glory, highly picturesque, but not great architecture, some of which contain good icons. And somewhere on the island is a church dedicated to the Drunken St. George, where the saint's name-day is said to be celebrated with nameless orgies but which, alas, I have never been able to find.

TENOS

Thanks to the discovery in 1822 of the miraculous icon of the Panaghia Teniotissa, the most celebrated and highly revered of any in Greece, Tenos has become the most popular place of pilgrimage in the orthodox world. The great church, a basilica of abnormal width designed for the accommodation of vast crowds of pilgrims, has little save its situation to commend it; it stands on the top of the hill, behind a quite pretty entrance gate decorated in a belated version of Turkish rococo, at the head of a wide, stepped street leading up from the waterfront, and commands good views over the harbour and neighbouring islands. The number of shops and booths selling holy medals, postcards and decorated candles, which surround it would seem to be even greater than those at Lourdes, and the quality of the wares displayed effectively demonstrates that, when it comes to pious knick-knacks, the Roman Catholics have nothing on the Orthodox.

Of the remaining Cyclades, almost all have one or two churches or monasteries which, if time allows, will well repay the trouble of a climb. Some of the best are to be found in the countryside on Siphnos, and the town churches on Mykonos are worth going into if only to get away from the prevailing atmosphere of hand-embroidered culture.

THE ASIA MINOR ISLANDS

CHIOS

Nea Moni. This splendid monastic church was founded by the Emperor Constantine Monomachus IX, and almost certainly built by a team of architects and workmen sent out from Constantinople between 1042 and 1056, and is thus a little later than Hosios Loukas and a little earlier than Daphni. The plan is octagonal but differs from that of its two near contemporaries in being inscribed directly in a square; here the squinches are carried straight across the corners from wall to wall, whereas in the other two they rest on L-shaped piers. The walls themselves, of which the marble revetment is still largely in situ, are divided into two zones by slightly projecting pilasters, from the summits of which spring the eight arches supporting the main dome. The exo-narthex has three domed bays and two projecting 'horse-shoe' apses of Anatolian type on the north and south; in the narthex itself, the two outer bays are covered with barrel vaults. Externally the decoration is comparatively simple, being confined to recessed niches and blind arcading in brick. It is not, however, to its architecture, splendid as it is, that Nea Moni chiefly owes its fame but to the great series of mosaics which cover most of the interior excepting the main dome.

Considering the fact that all three of the greatest remaining examples of mid-Byzantine mosaic decoration were carried out in very similar buildings within fifty years of each other, the stylistic differences between them are astonishing. Compared to those at Daphni, the present series seem rough and, save in the matter of colour, austere; whereas to the visitor coming straight from Hosios Loukas, the drawing, though harsh, may well appear sophisticated. It is, perhaps, by the modelling, particularly of the faces, that the artist of the Nea Moni chiefly impresses his personality.

Here are none of those delicate transitions of tone which softly round the features of the saints at Daphni; nor, on the other hand, is there any trace of that exclusive reliance on a largely linear technique, enlivened by rather arbitrary highlights, employed by his rival at Hosios Loukas. The contrast between light and shade is deliberately violent and the latter is used both to outline the figures and to intensify emotion, in fact exactly as it is employed by Rouault. To which of these three great masterpieces the visitor presents the palm will be determined by his temperamental reactions. But it cannot, I think, be denied that, at least in the matter of colour, the master of the Nea Moni has the edge on his contemporaries. Alongside these deep glowing blues, purples and crimsons, all intensified by the plain gold background unencumbered with landscape or architecture, the mosaics at Hosios Loukas and Daphni seem in retrospect to be inhibited, the first by a very restricted range, the second by a nervous restraint tending to over-refinement.

Where exactly the artists and craftsmen responsible hailed from remains a matter for conjecture. It would seem probable that, as the architect and builders almost certainly came from Constantinople, the mosaicists accompanied them; but, on the other hand, their achievement is of a completely different nature from that of any mosaics of this date existing in the capital. It seems just possible, therefore, that they came from some part of Southern Asia Minor, to the coast of which Chios is adjacent, untouched by the direct influence of the Imperial Court.

Of the other islands in this group, Mytilene is almost devoid of architectural interest, religious or secular, save for those wishing to study the influence of Belgian *art nouveau* on the later buildings of the Ottoman Empire. There is, however, in the strange inland village of Aigassos, a large basilical pilgrimage

church with a very celebrated icon in front of which devout ladies in very baggy Turkish trousers constantly prostrate themselves. Samos, on the other hand, has innumerable small churches perched on low hills, many with painted domes which, although individually of small importance, seen *en masse* give to certain of the island landscapes the look of a Goncharova back-drop.

THE DODECANESE

Rhodes

Thanks to the Fourth Crusade, to the Genoese and finally to the Knights of St. John of Jerusalem, the island of Rhodes was thoroughly gothicised during the long years which preceded the Turkish triumph. Subsequently the new arrivals set their own cultural stamp on the local architecture, and when they in their turn were ousted, the Italians soon embarked on a process of neo-gothicisation which culminated in prodigies of over-careful restoration combined, during the Fascist period, with an all-out attempt to revive the glories of Imperial Rome. It is not, therefore, very surprising that traces of Byzantium are few and far between.

Of the handful of churches and chapels which have survived, the most important is that on the Acropolis at Lindos, a ruined cross-in-square built of ashlar, with doubly recessed windows in the apses, usually a sign of Anatolian influence, dating from the Middle Byzantine period. In the lower town is another small church with singularly charming and well-preserved wall-paintings.

In the town of Rhodes are two churches, one, the Demirli Djami, dating from the same period, the other, the Khourmaly Medresse, slightly later. Both are ruinous and have been at some time or other used as mosques, and have domes resting on rather high, sixteen-sided drums. There is also a convent hard by the village of Eleoussa with 18th-century frescoes which I have not seen but have never heard of as being of any great beauty or interest.

Patmos

According to his own testimony St. John the Divine, or the Theologian as he is more generally referred to in Orthodox lands, wrote the Apocalypse 'when in the spirit on the Lord's Day' on the island of Patmos. The exact site of his labours, determined by venerable tradition, is a cave halfway up the mountain immediately behind the port, now incorporated in the small monastery of the Apocalypse. In the little church there are two aisles of which the southern is formed by the cave itself and is distinguished by a tripartite crack caused by the Voice of God, confirming the doctrine of the Trinity. Alongside it, protected by silver plates, is the spot where the Apostle rested his head. There is also in the north hall an early icon of St. Anne on the iconostasis.

In 1088 the whole island was granted by the Emperor Alexios Comnenos to the Blessed Chrystodoulos, a celebrated hermit who in due course founded the larger monastery, dedicated to S. Joannis Theologos on the Chora (as the cities of refuge perched aloft on inland peaks were generally called throughout the islands) which by the early 13th century had become an important foundation.

Of the original church only the narthex and exo-narthex remain; in the former are some admirable wall-paintings of the Macedonian school, dating from the early 15th century, but very hard to see, while those in the latter, which have recently been cleaned and over-restored, are provincial work of the 12th–13th century. The main body of the church was rebuilt in the second half of the 16th century, when the whole monastery was fortified, but the refectory, which contains fragments of 15th-century paintings, must date from an earlier rebuilding.

The adjacent library contains some world-famous manuscripts of outstanding quality and nearby, in a recently built gallery, is a magnificent collection of icons, some dating from as early as the 12th century. The site is that of a former temple of Artemis, some of the columns of which have been incorporated in the church, traditionally founded by Orestes in thanksgiving for his purification. The whole ensemble, although architecturally unremarkable, is highly picturesque and commands superb views.

THE ISLANDS OF THE SARONIC GULF

With the exception of Aegina, these islands were, throughout antiquity, supremely unimportant; they can boast few classical remains and received almost no contemporary mention. This state of isolation and neglect continued throughout Byzantine times, and it was not until the end of the 18th century that they emerged for the first time into history. During the course of the 17th century large areas of Greece, particularly in the Peloponnese and the neighbouring islands, had, due to the corruption and maladministration of the Turks, become completely depopulated, and in order to restore the balance, large numbers of Albanians, an energetic, and in their own country excessively troublesome, subject-race, were drafted southwards. Of these the most enterprising were those colonising the island of Hydra, who, faced with the impossibility of scratching a living on that uncultivable rock, took to the sea and became the best shipbuilders and navigators in the Aegean.

During Nelson's blockade of the Mediterranean the local captains amassed large fortunes running cargoes from the Levant to Marseilles and Leghorn, and on their retirement built for themselves noble palazzi in a massive, local style which derived ultimately from the buildings put up by the Venetians in Nauplion just across the straits. During the War of Independence the Magnates of Hydra, thanks to their wealth and their fleet, played a decisive role, but in the years which followed, the importance of the island declined at a rate which was much accelerated by the coming of steam and the subsequent development of the shipping industry in Chios. Today, for most of the year, it shelters a population far smaller than that for which the town was built, and only in summer, when there regularly descends an army of international trippers and refugees from St. Tropez, does the island display a certain trendy animation.

HYDRA

The principal place of worship is the church of the monastery of the Panaghia on the port, said to have been founded in the 17th century but heavily restored and much enlarged in the 18th and 19th. A domed basilica, with an exo-narthex on pointed arches standing in the middle of a large arcaded courtyard, it is of no great architectural importance, but the interior is of interest for the large number of costly ex-votos with which successful captains took pride in adorning it, the most fascinating of which is, perhaps, a large candelabra in gilded bronze decorated with fleurs-de-lis, looted from the Tuileries in 1792. The campanile is 19th century and said to have been copied from one on Mykonos.

In the upper town are two small churches one of which—a cross-in-square painted pink externally and dedicated, I think, to Hagios Georgios—has some rather nice late wall-paintings with dark blue backgrounds and animated figures. The nervous are warned that the best place from which to view them, the women's gallery at the west end, is, or was when I was last there, ankle-deep in skulls and bones.

On the summit of the mountain are the twin monasteries of the Prophet Elias, one male, one female, which it is claimed were founded by a refugee monk from Athos who fled to Hydra. While it is just possible, but unlikely, that their foundation dates from this period (late 15th century) both are in their present state almost entirely of the last century, and the latter, inhabited by embroidery-hawking nuns, exceptionally ugly.

There are one or two more monasteries on the island, none of great interest, and a number of small chapels, the prettiest of which is that on the tiny promontory of Vlikos, a mile or so to the west of the town.

SPETSAI

In the pinewoods behind the town, which is a rather genteel Victorian version of Hydra, very popular as a holiday resort with 'toute Athènes', is a small monastic church with pleasant unsophisticated wall-paintings very late in date. Otherwise nothing.

POROS

Another holiday island, attracting a rather more middle-class public than Spetsai, it has one charmingly situated monastery dedicated to the Panaghia, alongside a spring overshadowed by gigantic planes, about three miles from the town, conveniently close to the last bus stop. The church, which was founded in the 18th century by a Metropolitan of Athens who had been cured of the stone by the waters of the spring, has an arcaded exo-narthex which contains a memorial plaque to an unfortunate young ensign of Her Majesty's Foot Guards, who here succumbed to a fever in 1828, while serving as military attaché in Athens.

AEGINA

S. Nikolaos is the first church one sees on arriving by sea, situated on the end of one of the two moles encircling the harbour. It was erected early in the 19th century by refugees from Chios in thanksgiving for their salvation from shipwreck; with twin domes and heavily whitewashed, it has in these surroundings a surprisingly Cycladic look.

The Monastery of the Phanoromeni is situated a short distance from the town on the road up to the temple. Enclosed in monastic buildings dating from the 18th century, the remains of an early basilica with three apses, enriched externally with niches, are still standing. A little further on, a path leads to the Omorphi Ekklesia (the Beautiful Church), dedicated to the Two Theodores which was built in 1282 and contains frescoes some of which are still in quite good condition.

Palaeochora is a ruined city of refuge erected in mediaeval times and subsequently abandoned when the coastal capital once more became reasonably safe. Clinging to the slopes of the mountain are a dozen or more churches in varying stages of dilapidation, mostly dating from the 13th century, many of which are said to contain stone screens, frescoes and decorative sculpture of considerable interest.

CRETE

Proximity to the north coast of Africa, comparative fertility and size have all combined to render the history of Crete rather different from that of any of the other islands. In Roman times it was included in the province of Cyrenaica of which the Capital was at Gortyna, and was among the earliest centres of Christianity, in the Empire, outside Palestine. According to tradition the first Bishop of Gortyna was Titus, appointed by his friend the Apostle Paul. After the division of the Empire it naturally passed into Byzantine hands in which it remained until, in A.D. 828, it was captured by the Arabs, who held it for over a century. In A.D. 961 it was finally regained for the Empire by Nicephorus Phocas, but after the Fourth Crusade it passed to the Venetians, who were not relieved of it by the Turks until 1669.

Of the innumerable churches and chapels with which the island is covered, only two, both ruined, can with any degree of probability be assigned to the first Byzantine period and not many, in their present state, to the second. Under the Venetians, however, who do not appear to have interfered in any marked degree with the religious life of the Greek inhabitants, the island enjoyed great prosperity that found expression in widespread church-

140

The Panaghia Kera, Kritsa

building, in a style which, while remaining basically Byzantine, was, to a certain extent, particularly in matters of detail, influenced by the Gothic, and later Renaissance, buildings erected by the ruling class. Thus one is continually being surprised by the discovery of ogival windows and Gothic cusping in a firmly Byzantine apse, and even more frequently by rather depressing attempts to adjust the traditional layout of the Greek icon to a Renaissance conception of space. In the wall-paintings, however, the highly developed Cretan tradition remained largely unmodified.

Of the two Capitals of the island, Heraklion—one of the very few ports in the Aegean that is totally devoid of character—possesses few buildings of any antiquity, and these few are Venetian. In the restored church of S. Mark there is a small collection of Cretan-Byzantine wall-paintings. Khania, on the other hand, is highly picturesque and adorned with the remains of a large number of palazzi and several Renaissance churches, but here, too, Byzantine architecture is virtually unrepresented. The hinterland, however, is for the amateur Byzantinist *terra incognita*; only a small proportion of the chapels and churches, tucked away in gorges, isolated on forgotten plateaux, seldom of major architectural importance but of which a surprisingly large number have paintings of considerable quality, are mentioned in the guide-books, and still fewer described.

Most of the larger monasteries, of which that on the headland of Akrotiri is typical, have been frequently rebuilt and in their present state can hardly qualify as Byzantine works.

EPISKOPI

To the south of Khania, among the foothills and gorges of the White Mountains, are a number of small churches of which the most interesting is that at Episkopi. Centrally planned, with barrel-vaulted aisles opening into the narthex, it is crowned with a very shallow dome, lacking a drum but raised on a couple of steps like a miniature Pantheon. This, together with the fact that it was formerly the seat of an archbishop, and with the presence in the north aisle of a sunken cruciform font, encourages the belief that it is a very early foundation indeed, dating from the first period of Byzantine rule. However, as it is not mentioned in any of the standard works, and at the time of my only visit appeared to be totally deserted, this judgement remains personal. The only human being in sight on that occasion was a small boy, busily chasing a family of rats along the top of the iconostasis, who was not helpful.

ALIKIANOU

A small church with very interesting paintings in a highly personal style, well 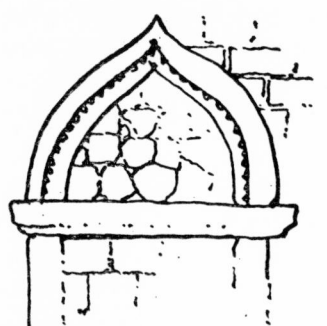 worth a great deal more care and attention than they were receiving two years ago. Near-by, beyond the charming village of Theorissou, are two small churches in a dilapidated but picturesque state. One, very tiny, with almost invisible wall-paintings and, in the west wall, a curious ogival supporting arch surmounting a flat lintel, a very characteristic indication of Venetian influence; the other, a cross-in-square, a plan far less common here than on the main-land, with the dome supported on three columns with re-used classical capitals and a single square unadorned pier.

GORTYNA

The basilica of Titus, midway on the road between Heraklion and Phaestos, is not only the oldest church on the island, but one which proves the exception to the rule that Byzantine churches do not make good ruins. All that remains is the sanctuary with flanking chapels, but this is of such a height as to dominate, and provide a focal point for, the typical, rather Claude-like, landscape of tumbled Roman ruins engulfed in olives. Originally a large basilica, with much in common with the near-contemporary church on Paros, it possessed transepts, aisles and narthex, today represented only by their foundations. Apart from their height, the sanctuary and adjoining chapels are also distinguished by their plan, polygonal on the outside, triconch within.

POTAMIES

To the east of Heraklion the main-road runs along the coast to Agios Nikolaos; rather less than halfway, a smaller road leads off to the right up to the extraordinary windmill-dotted plateau of Lassithi. Just before the stiff climb begins, lies the village of Potamies with, a mile outside it, the church of the Panaghia Goberniotissa, of which the key is in the keeping of an enthusiastic French-speaking *pappas* living in the village itself.

Cruciform in plan, the crossing is surmounted by a circular drum with shallow blind arcading round the windows. The only signs of Venetian influence are a small quatrefoil window and a pointed supporting arch over

the main door, both in the west wall. Inside are some very good paintings, but not, alas, in very good condition, of which the most notable is a charming 'Three Marys at the Tomb', with a very beautifully painted angel on the north wall of the west aisle, and a first-rate Pantokrator in the dome. There are also some splendid Emperors and Empresses, all in full fig complete with haloes, and the remains of a Dormition on the west wall. Both the paintings and the church itself are probably of the 14th century.

Kritsa

On the other side of the plateau, where the mountains begin to fall away to the Gulf of Mirabello, is the largest village on the island, Kritsa, a single street running along the mountainside with several small Byzantine churches of which the most noteworthy are the Panaghia Kera and S. Nikolaos. The former, which stands a little outside the village, has aisles very wide for their length, and a dome supported internally on four superimposed ribs which clearly date from some later rebuilding. The aisles, which are similarly roofed, are supported externally by buttresses. In the west façade are two strange little pointed windows in which a rather wild attempt to achieve a Gothic effect by cusping suggest that they, too, date from the period of the rebuilding.

The wall-paintings, which, although repainted here and there, are basically 14th century, are splendid and very different in feeling from contemporary examples of the Macedonian school, much darker in tone and far more linear in treatment. (Compare the scene of Herod and Salome here with the handling of the same scene in the Panaghia Koubedeliki in Kastoria.) There are remains of a Doom on the west wall and two very fine but incomplete equestrian saints. On the barrel-vaulting of the *naos* is the Nativity, and a good Pantokrator, almost life-size, stands to the south of the Holy Door. Everywhere there are sensitively rendered heads, one of the best being that of a tonsured saint in what would seem to be Franciscan habit—the rope round the waist is still clearly discernible—perhaps St. Francis himself; if this is so, it must be the saint's only appearance in Byzantine iconography. The remaining paintings in the central aisle would seem to be later in date, although not very much. In the north apse, extending westward into the aisle, are long rows of saints and angels grouped behind the seated apostles, their multicoloured haloes overlapping and extending in an illusory perspective into the background. Also in the north aisle are two very good Donor portraits, a feature much less common here than in the north of Greece and in Cyprus.

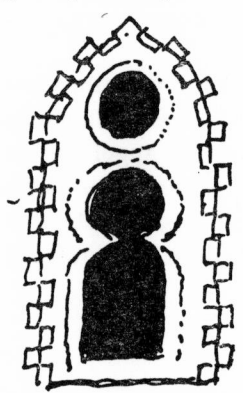

144

S. Nikolaos is a simple oblong in plan, divided by an arch between the *naos* and *bema*. The paintings, which are almost as good as those in the Panaghia, are characterised by a similar reliance on a firm, dark outline; the finest are the two very splendid figures in court dress standing on either side of the dividing arch.

7

ASIA MINOR

URING the reign of Justinian, when Byzantine power enjoyed
its furthest extension, Asia Minor was the very heartland of the
Empire. Not only did it contain the greatest of those Hellenistic
centres of civilisation wherein a distinctively Byzantine, as opposed to neo-
classical, culture had first developed, but the Anatolian plateau was for the
Byzantines what Central Africa was in our time for the French—'un reservoir
d'hommes'. Less than 200 years after Justinian's death a dim, Semitic tribe
from the south of the Arabian peninsula, God-inspired, overran almost the
whole Mediterranean complex in a matter of years. From the Nile to the
Rhône, from Spain to the borders of Afghanistan, the ancient world had
succumbed overnight; Micklegarth itself held firm, just, but vast territories
on which it had previously relied for support, both economical and military,
were rapidly absorbed. One by one the great cities of antiquity—Alexandria,
Jerusalem, Damascus, Antioch—fell to the infidel, until at last the invaders
were clamouring outside the Theodosian walls. Given the history of these
provinces it is hardly surprising that today little exists from the high Byzantine period except in almost total decay, and that later building is small-scale
and fragmentary. Ruins are numerous, but in most cases, while possibly
rating alpha plus for historical interest, can hardly be accorded more than
beta minus for aesthetic value. In what is now Turkey, there is the great
church at Trebizond (alas, unseen by me); the rock churches of Cappadocia
of which the paintings are of seminal importance, but of which the construction would seem to be of speleological rather than architectural interest;
a number of isolated monasteries and churches on that most beautiful of
lakes, Lake Barfa, which, judging by the masonry, date from the 12th or 13th
centuries (and in the hills behind which no one, so far as I know, has ever
climbed, allegedly a number of small painted churches of the same period);
and one ruin of such importance that despite my proviso it cannot pass un-
mentioned.

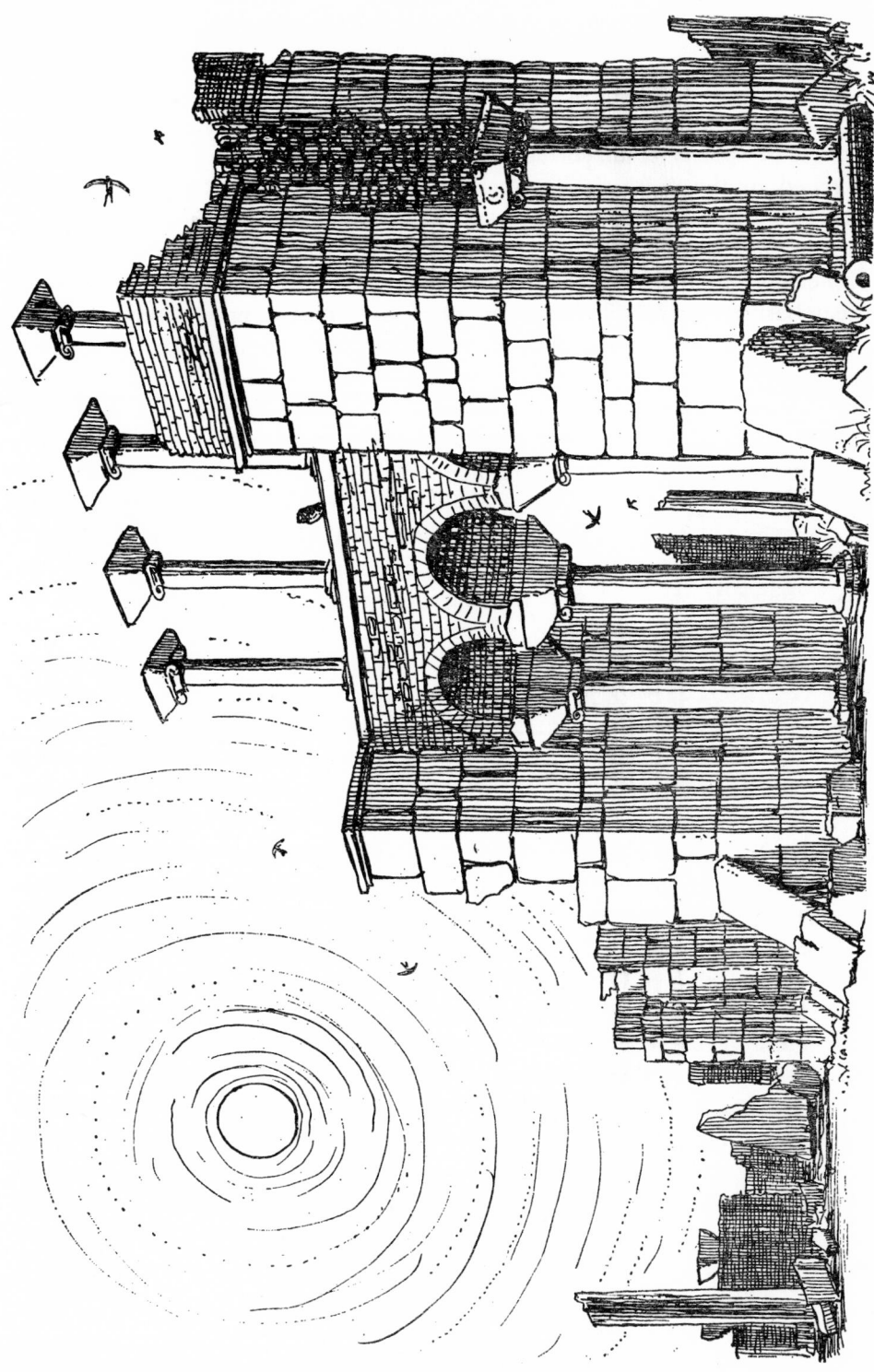

That the great basilica of S. John the Divine at Ephesus is not today a total ruin is largely due to Mr. George B. Quatman of Lima, Ohio, and the American Society of the Friends of Ephesus who have for some time been engaged in the aesthetically questionable activity of restoration. Thanks largely to their industry, while it remains doubtful whether the appearance of the site has been improved, the plan and layout are now readily comprehensible. For this we should be duly grateful, as it seems likely that this great basilica, as rebuilt by Justinian, approximated more closely than any other building to the Church of the Holy Apostles in Constantinople of which the contemporary influence was so widespread. While the five domes, the apse, the galleries and most of the pillars screening the aisles have all vanished, their position is easily determined, and the whole architectural conception is, perhaps, more easily to be comprehended than it is at S. Mark's, where it is

difficult to see the original wood for the number and complexity of the alien trees. The scale and proportions are clearly superb, but the detail, judging by the remaining capitals, of which the clumsiness is hardly redeemed by the presence of the entwined monograms of Justinian and Theodora, is surprisingly poor. However, there still exists, although roofless, a charming octagonal baptistry on the north side with engaged pillars in the angles. A little further to the east, is a small painted chapel of later date, where the flaking away of the superimposed layers of repainting on the figures of the saints enables one to appreciate just how far the original contours of a Byzantine painting were liable to fluctuate in the course of time.

From the reign of Constantine onwards it was naturally the Holy Land itself that witnessed the greatest building activity, but of all the shrines, churches and martyria which succeeded each other on the sacred sites, little enough that is specifically Byzantine remains today. Of the plan and layout of the Holy Sepulchre as finally reorganised by Justinian, it is now impossible to form any just impression, so great is the darkness and confusion, so haphazard and distracting the additions and enclosures whereby the competing sects have sought to establish their independence and importance, and the only stylistic note that is clearly and unmistakably sounded is that of French Romanesque. At Bethlehem, although the air is still heavy with commercial

piety, and the tide of *bondieuseries* runs almost as high, the main lines and proportions of the four-aisled basilica, with apse-ended transepts and roofed in
timber, with which Justinian replaced the Church erected by Constantine,
are easily to be appreciated, although very little of the original decoration
has survived and the existing mosaics all date from the 12th century.

Ironically enough, the erection of the two most impressive Byzantine monuments in all Syria was due not to the Greeks but to their conquerors. The
Ommayads, the earliest rulers of the vast Arab dominions, are among the
most attractive dynasties known to history. Cultured, tolerant and self-
indulgent, their devotion to the austerer elements of the Moslem creed was not
marked. Although only a generation away from the black tents, and pos-
sessing no artistic traditions whatever, they were from the first fully apprecia-
tive of the luxury and cultural achievements of their new subjects, and did not
allow religious considerations to stand in the way of fruitful collaboration.
Greek artists from Antioch and Damascus were called in to decorate their
palaces—one of the most beautiful of all Byzantine secular mosaics is a
pavement in the Ommayad hunting lodge at Jericho—and even their
mosques. Whether or not the Dome of the Rock is the work of Byzantine
architects, the plan, a central dome supported on an inner ring of pillars
surrounded by an octagonal ambulatory, was certainly Greek inspired; and
the mosaic decoration of the rich, gold acanthus scrolls (even the broad-
minded Ommayads could not permit representation in this, the second
holiest spot in all Islam) we know to have been carried out by specially commissioned designers from Constantinople.

In Damascus the ancient temple of Jupiter had, according to some
accounts, been converted by Theodosius I to Christian worship. Others
maintain that, while the general layout of the temple area was retained, the
actual basilica was a Theodosian rebuilding. Whatever its origin, the existing
structure was transformed by the Ommayads into a mosque, a change that
involved a complete right-angle reorientation. However, it is not the mosque
itself, but the surrounding arcaded open space, which holds our interest today.
The northern wall was covered by indisputably Greek workmen with a
wonderful continuous mosaic landscape, diversified with architecture but
unenlivened, for obvious doctrinal reasons, by figures. The overall effect, as
it survives today, owes something to the old classical tradition of 'veduti', as
represented both in Pompeii itself and in the Naples Museum; something to the
late Roman illuminated decorative estate maps carried out in mosaic, of
which a large selection are visible in the Bardo Museum in Tunis; and—is it

too far-fetched to suggest?—possibly something to the landscape scrolls being produced contemporaneously in far-away, but not unattainable, China. Whatever its inspirational origins, it remains one of the most magical imaginary landscapes created by man.

CYPRUS

In the division of the Empire, the island of Cyprus naturally passed to the East and, with the organisation of Christianity, was made subject ecclesiastically to the Patriarchate of Antioch. The relationship between the Archbishop of Constantia (Salamis) and the Patriarch was not, however, a happy one, and in A.D. 477 a most fortunate discovery enabled the former to establish his complete independence. In that year the body of St. Barnabas, himself a Cypriot, was found miraculously preserved, together with a copy of the Gospel according to St. Matthew in the disciple's own handwriting. Very sensibly the Archbishop went straightway to Constantinople where he presented the manuscript to the Emperor Zeno—taking care to point out that this, of course, made nonsense of the Patriarch's claim that the Word had first come to the island from Antioch—who was so impressed that in order suitably to mark his gratitude he granted the Archbishop complete independence from any Patriarchal supervision as sole ruler of an autocephalous church, together with numerous other privileges such as that of signing documents in the Imperial purple ink (a position which all his successors have continued to enjoy down to the present day).

Once established, the island's close connection with Capital and Court continued until the Arab invasions in the 7th century, which accounts for the very high quality of what little art has survived from that period. With the coming of the infidels, whose raids were constant and prolonged, almost all contact with the rest of the Empire was severed for well over 200 years. However, this enforced isolation had one advantage, for so hard was the Church's struggle for survival that no surplus energy was available for theological debate, and the island was spared the worst excesses of the iconoclastic controversy. Fortunately, while the Arabs were not only infinitely destructive but also, anyhow in theory, the sworn foes of representational art, they were not fired by the same zeal as the Iconoclasts, which may well account for the survival of the island's two very early mosaics of the Panaghia. (Perhaps some among the invaders may have been uneasily aware that a painting of the Virgin Mary existed in the Mosque of the Kaaba in Mecca itself.)

After the power of the Arabs had finally been broken by Nicephorus Phocas' recapture of Crete, the life of the island gradually returned to normal, and if there is little evidence of the artistic influence of the Macedonian Renaissance, no part of the Empire, certainly not the Capital, can boast of more or finer examples of the art of the Comnenian epoch.

In the pre-invasion period, the majority of the Cypriot churches were basilical and, with the resumption of building, the same plan was usually followed with, however, one important modification; previously the basilicas had been roofed in timber, now they were barrel-vaulted with one, two or even three domes arranged longitudinally. Examples of both the fully developed cross-in-square and the octagonal plan exist, but are far rarer than on the mainland.

From the time of the island's capture by Richard Coeur-de-Lion until the final victory of the Turks, architecture and painting were constantly exposed to Western influence. Architecturally the principal result was the widespread adoption of the pointed arch. With the establishment of the Lusignan dynasty, the relationship between Latins and Orthodox, which had, until then, been highly embittered, improved, and fraternisation was often carried to the length of intermarriage, and Latin chapels were regularly attached to Orthodox churches. Of this short-lived period the most elaborate monument is, perhaps, the Cathedral of S. George of the Greeks in Famagusta where ogival vaults and a Gothic feeling for height were combined with a dome and wholly Greek wall-paintings; but the most characteristic is the accepted model for dozens of the smaller Cypriot churches, a domed rectangle with arched recesses north and south, a high drum and a projecting apse, the whole roofed with a lime and mortar cement.

Under the Turks, building languished here as elsewhere; only towards the end of their period of rule did a certain modest activity manifest itself, which resulted in the emergence of a type of architecture peculiar to Cyprus. The single-aisled basilica persisted but, while the domes and their dividing bays were both abandoned, the supporting lateral vaults were retained, with the result that the external appearance of the church resembled that of a high, vaulted barn, its long roof flanked by rows of contiguous dormers. With the coming of the British this austerity was modified by the addition of campaniles; the Turks, justifiably nervous of a possible 'tocsin', had forbidden belfries altogether. Now, as an expression of their new-found freedom, the Cypriots proceeded to erect campaniles all over the island, most of them in a very fancy version of Levantine neo-Gothic.

LYTHRANKOMI

The church of the Panaghia Kanakaria as it exists today is a building of many periods; the apse is all that remains of a very early basilica destroyed by the Arabs; the aisles were added but not fully incorporated in the structure during a subsequent rebuilding; later, in the 11th century, a dome was constructed over the nave and in the 12th a domed narthex was attached to the west end. However, the total effect is happy and the whole building, viewed from without, composes admirably. Within, the great treasure of the church is the fragmentary mosaic in the conch of the apse. This, which has been the subject of much learned dispute, is, or was, a depiction of the Virgin between archangels with the Child on her knees, a characteristically Cypriot arrangement. Today all that remains is the Child Himself and the head of one archangel, and the immediate effect has been much diminished by recent would-be-helpful repainting. (Why can restorers not leave well alone and indicate the ascertainable missing portions of a mosaic such as this by simple outlines in grisaille?) Both the figure of the Child and the head of the angel suggest a very early date; the tesserae are large (far larger than those at Khiti), and the whole has a distinctly archaic, but certainly not primitive, air, an impression which is reinforced by the heads of the apostles in roundels decorating the soffit of the encompassing arch, which recall similar works in Rome and Ravenna. These subjective arguments for an early date are supported by theological pronouncements; at the Council of Ephesus in A.D. 431 the status of the Virgin was, once and for all, established as 'Theotokos', the Mother of God; her presence here in a 'mandorla', very rare, and with attendant archangels, would, therefore, suggest a date fairly soon after the definitive confirmation of the dogma. However, some attribute the work to a far later period, basing their arguments on a fancied resemblance to some of the Sicilian mosaics at Palermo, a theory which seems to me hardly sustainable.

KHITI

The Church of the Panaghia Angeloktistos (Built-by-the-Angels) is a domed cruciform, typically Cypriot in appearance, with a single-aisled, rib-vaulted Latin chapel, its main door heraldically embellished, attached to the south

side, and with a small domed Byzantine chapel on the north. Originally it was a basilica, dating probably from the 6th century and destroyed by the Arabs, of which today only the central apse remains. Fortunate, indeed, that it does, for it contains what is certainly the greatest single work of art on the island—a mosaic of the Virgin and Child between two archangels on a plain gold ground. The Virgin, who is described, most unusually at this date, as Hagia Maria, is standing full face with the Child on her left arm in a slightly swaying stance, emphasised by the outward swing of her dark crimson cloak, which immediately recalls the Imperial portraits at Ravenna. The heads of the attendant archangels, who are shown in half-profile doing reverence to the central figure, are most delicately drawn and modelled and the treatment of Gabriel's robes beautifully reinforces the underlying rhythm of the whole group (those of Michael have largely disappeared). Around the curve of the conch extends an elaborate border of acanthus scrolls, birds and stags' heads, only recently uncovered. When I first saw this wonderful work twenty years ago it came as a complete surprise; at that time it was barely, if ever, mentioned in most of the standard works and no reproductions were available. Today, while its beauty seldom receives its rightful recognition, its art-historical importance is generally accepted, and has given rise to much controversy. Although it has been held by some to be a work of the 11th century, a far earlier date is now generally, and in my view correctly, suggested. The high quality of workmanship and the resemblance to certain of the Ravenna mosaics, both of the figures and certain details of the surrounding border, would unquestionably seem to support the theory that it is a work of the 6th century. After this great masterpiece the few remaining paintings, both in the church itself, and in the northern annex, seem very small beer.

SALAMIS AND LARNACA

The two great churches of S. Barnabas at Salamis and S. Lazarus at Larnaca are historically important but aesthetically unrewarding. The former marks the spot where the disciple's corpse was so conveniently discovered by Archbishop Anthemios in the 5th century, but was almost entirely rebuilt in the 18th. It retains, however, three domes over the nave, replacing an original wooden roof.

The latter, also three-domed, marks the final sepulchre of Lazarus, who, after his restoration to life, ended up in Cyprus and became its first bishop. Although various classical and Byzantine capitals have been incorporated into the existing structure, which dates from a 17th-century rebuilding, the interior is supremely uninteresting save for those with a passion for religious *boiseries*. The campanile, which is large and decorated with extraordinary neo-Levantine-Gothic plate tracery, is of interest as being almost the only one that the Turks permitted to be built during their period of sovereignty.

S.ᵗ Chrysostomos, Koutsovendis.

KOUTSOVENDIS

The monastery of S. Chrysostomos at Koutsovendis, behind Bellapais, possesses a double church; the larger structure, of which the foundation dates from the 10th century, is an almost entirely modern rebuilding of small importance, but the other, dedicated to the Holy Trinity, is of the highest interest. The plan conforms to the usual Cypriot pattern but the material in which it is carried out is brick, a rare occurrence on the island and, what is rarer still, the brickwork is of extremely high quality. According to an inscription recently uncovered, the church was founded at the end of the 10th century by the Duke-Governor of Cyprus, which possibly explains the high quality of the work and the strongly metropolitan character of the paintings. These are, at the moment, fragmentary but it is to be hoped that after the restoration that is now being carried out by the Byzantine Institute of Dumbarton Oaks, more will be revealed. At present, a number of saints, two in monastic garb, are clearly visible in the *bema*, together with, on the north wall, a very beautiful fragment of an Anastasis showing an animated John the Baptist with Solomon and David. But the finest paintings that have so far been recovered are undoubtedly the heads of saints in roundels, including one of S. Demetrios in a straight Beatle haircut, decorating the soffit of the north-west recess, which are as fine as anything of the period to be found anywhere.

A few yards down the hill is the ruined church of the Panaghia Aphendrika where, on the outside of the north wall, are some fragments of an Epitaphios which, to judge from the beauty of the wonderfully drawn heads of the mourning Marys, must have been an outstanding masterpiece of the 12th century. Inside, right of the west entrance, are the remains of a very spirited St. George of a later period; the Saint's head has disappeared but not, fortunately, that of the delightful Victorian rocking-horse on which he is mounted, nor one shapely and richly clad leg of the coffee boy astride behind him.

The Monastery of Christ Antiphonitis. This disused monastery is situated in a steep and wooded valley near the village of Kalagreia. Dating from the 12th century it is one of the only two churches on the island conforming to the contemporary octagonal plan so popular on the Greek mainland. The other is the chapel in the castle of Hilarion which, though roofless and ruinous, is rather better proportioned. Here the square has been reduced to a regular

SS. Barnabas and Hilarion, Peristerona

octagon by eight circular piers, four engaged with the walls, two semi-detached, and two free-standing; a rather hamfisted version of the layout adopted in the great church at Nea Moni on Chios. Externally the church, although extremely picturesque, suggests a rustic and clumsy version of Daphni. The vaulted narthex, a 14th-century addition, has pointed arches, as has an open loggia, once roofed in wood, along the south wall. Inside there are two series of paintings, neither in very good condition; the earlier,

confined to the *bema* and the apse, are contemporary with the building of the church, the rest dating from the 15th century. Of the former, the most impressive, although badly damaged, are the Virgin and attendant angel in the half-dome (at the time of my last visit undergoing much needed repairs and very difficult to see) and a couple of half-length stylites perched on carefully railed-in pillar-tops. The Tree of Jesse, a subject less frequent here than in Western Christendom, on the south wall, and the Last Judgement opposite, both belonging to the latter series, are accomplished but not very inspired. The Pantokrator in the dome is large without being impressive.

PERACHORIO

The Church of the Holy Apostles, just off the main road from Nicosia to Limassol, is a squat but charming little building with a single aisle and a drumless dome dating from the second half of the 12th century. Architecturally unremarkable, the wall-paintings which are contemporary with the

church are, although badly damaged, sophisticated and of a high quality. While there are few traces of that Hellenism so apparent in contemporary work elsewhere on the island, the style is not yet markedly Eastern-Monastic. In the half-dome of the apse is the Panaghia between SS. Peter and Paul; immediately below is the Communion of the Apostles; on the lowest tier are saints and Church Fathers. Notice particularly the very beautiful figure of the communicating apostle on the right, whose robes are drawn with an extraordinary flickering quality of line, reminiscent of some of the Anglo-Saxon illuminations of the Winchester school. In the tier immediately below, the paint has flaked away from some of the heads, notably those on the north, revealing an under-painting in sanguine, that powerfully reinforces the theory that even the most stylised art, if good, rests on a solidly naturalistic basis. In the dome is the Pantokrator, damaged, surrounded by angels of which the best preserved is of an exceptional beauty. Elsewhere in the church is a Nativity which, although by a less accomplished hand, includes a notably charming group of two shepherds.

TRIKOMO

S. James. This enchanting little building is, perhaps, the prettiest and most typical of all the smaller Cypriot churches. Free-standing in the village square, built, probably, some time in the 15th century, it is a simple domed

rectangle with pointed arches supporting a high drum, with arched recesses on the inside of the north and south walls, and pointed hood-mouldings over the doors. There are no paintings and internally the only decoration is provided by a series of rather pretty dishes of local pottery set in the apse and side walls. When I first saw this church it was bound round with a tightly knotted rope, a very ancient, and now I imagine completely abandoned, method of warning travellers that the village was in the grip of an infectious disease.

The Panaghia Theotokos. This, the main church of the village, was probably erected in the 12th century on the usual domed basilical plan, but in the 15th century a vaulted aisle was added on the north, separated from the nave by a pair of wide, very low-span arches with Gothic mouldings which create a very bizarre effect. At the same time the church was extended towards the west. The Virgin in the apse is a 15th-century repainting, but in the vault above is a Christ Ascending surrounded by a circle of very dashing airborne angels dating from the 12th century. In the dome a rather despondent Pantokrator is encircled by a splendidly rendered angelic host advancing from two directions, headed by the Panaghia and John the Baptist, eastwards towards the Hetoimasia. In the main vault of the 15th-century addition is a painting of Christ in an aureole, which shows strong and unwelcome Western influence. Elsewhere there is also a group of three shepherds, one playing the *flute-à-travers* the wrong way round, which is all that remains of a vanished Nativity.

PERISTERONA

The Church of S. Barnabas and S. Hilarion is of considerable interest as being the best existing example of the final development of a church plan peculiar to Cyprus; it is also very beautiful. A basilica with barrel-vaulted aisles divided from the nave, not by pillars, but by solid walls pierced with arched openings and with three projecting apses, it is covered, as at S. Barnabas and S. Lazarus, by three domes arranged longitudinally, of which that in the centre is here flanked by two smaller domes set over the aisles. Viewed externally the plan produces an effect not dissimilar to that achieved by the five-domed churches of earlier times such as the Holy Apostles at Constantinople and S. Marco in Venice, with which, in fact, it has no connection whatever. The interior is not absorbingly interesting, having been heavily restored on more than one occasion, and nothing remains of the original 11th-century decoration, but there are a few fragments of later wall-paintings of small merit, a good pair of painted and gilded gates, on the north of the iconostasis in an Italo-Byzantine style, one or two interesting icons and some superb wooden doors in the west entrance. At some time during the last twenty years considerable tarting-up of the exterior has taken place, producing the usual depressing effect; formerly the three main domes were covered with tiles and the apses with crumbling plaster; now the former are protected by nice, smooth cement, and the stonework of the latter has been thoroughly scraped and neatly repointed.

LAMBOUSA

The monastery of the Panaghia Achiropoitos (Not-built-with-hands), is an ancient foundation which, in its present form, dates largely from the 15th century. Picturesquely situated on the edge of the sea, it is surrounded by

arcaded cells on two floors formerly inhabited by stray shepherds, farm animals and English intellectuals. Now, alas, it has been taken over by the army and one can only view the remains accompanied by a suspicious and resentful Greek conscript.

The main body of the church itself has two domes and dates from the 14th century; later, an enormous apse, totally out of proportion with the nave and *bema*, was added, which gives the whole a very bizarre appearance. A little later still, a narthex and exo-narthex in the Gothic style were built on to the west end. Internally the church is of little interest but it has, or had, a very fine marble floor.

THE TROODOS

When, after Richard Coeur-de-Lion's capture of Cyprus, the Latins moved in en masse, they lost no time in liberating the richest foundations and most profitable benefices from the schismatics. As a result, the Orthodox were driven away from the fertile centre of the island, and tended to congregate in the high and unattractive mountain range in the south-west, that already sheltered several small monasteries, where they erected a number of churches, small in scale but architecturally unique. At first they simply repeated the domed cruciform model which had by now become standard practice, but soon discovered that in this new environment it was structurally inadequate; the multiplicity of planes involved in its roof construction, while presenting no problems in the dry hot plain, here in the mountains annually collected deep pockets of snow. The solution of this problem remains an admirable example of architectural empiricism; the whole church was covered with a pitched roof, with very wide eaves, resting either on a newly built surrounding wall, or on vertical extensions of the existing walls, with the eaves supported by a wooden arcade often closed with grilles. In either case this resulted in the church itself being surrounded by a continuous ambulatory or outer passage. In some cases, where the drum of the dome was too high to be accommodated easily under a continuous roof, it was allowed to poke through, and was itself protected by a small additional roof.

The excessively rustic appearance of the majority of these churches which, seen from without, resemble small Swiss chalets, is deceptive; the internal decoration is almost always elaborate and frequently highly sophisticated, and the frescoes are often of a quality that stands comparison with the very best contemporary work existing anywhere in the Empire. Indeed, taken as a whole, the wall-paintings of the Troodos seem to me far superior to those on Athos and, given the difference in style and date, every bit as impressive as those of Mistra.

Of the twenty or more churches in this group I have selected half a dozen which seem to me the best and most characteristic.

KAKOPETRIA

S. Nicholas of the Roofs (Hagios Nikolaos tis Steyis), of which the foundation preceded the coming of the Franks by a century or more, is a cross-in-square, more closely related to contemporary work in Greece itself than any other on the island, carried out by masons who seem to have had rather a hazy idea of exactly what they were supposed to be doing, to which a narthex with cupola was added in the 12th century. In the 13th, the whole building was covered with a pitched roof, probably the first time that this characteristic device was employed in the region. The paintings with which the church is covered internally range from the early 11th century to the 17th and include some of the finest in Cyprus. The earliest, which are very beautiful and intense, are amongst the only local examples of the work of the Macedonian Renaissance; particularly fine, and markedly hieratic, are the Transfiguration and the Raising of Lazarus. Of the 12th-century paintings in the narthex, the most interesting is the personification of the sea, a naked maiden riding a sea monster, a straight hangover from the late classical world. Notice that she is portrayed in profile with only one eye visible, indicating that she was most definitely not a subject for veneration. The superb pair of archangels, also in the narthex, are slightly later in date, as are the Crucifixion and the Anastasis. Of the remainder of the paintings, dating from the 14th century onwards, there is none which can compare in quality with the earlier work, although in the 14th-century Nativity there is a charming little bagpipe-playing shepherd and a nice goat.

NIKITARI (ASINOU)

The church of the Panaghia Phorbiotissa is a single-aisled building with a barrel vault reinforced by transverse arches, and with arched recesses on north and south, dating from the early 12th century. The narthex, which is a later addition, has a domed cupola and apsidal ends which project beyond the outer wall supporting the usual overall roof. Of the wall-paintings, which are complete and, on the whole, very impressive, a very beautiful Communion of the Apostles, with a particularly moving portrait of our Lord regarding the departing Judas, dates from the foundation of the church, as does the outstanding Dormition of the Virgin on the west wall. Not only is the latter one of the earliest but also one of the most beautiful renderings of this theme in Byzantine art; particularly striking is the dramatic treatment of the group of mourning apostles at the foot of the bier, among whom St. Paul, in the foreground, bears a strong resemblance to his almost contemporary portrayal in St. Anselm's Chapel in Canterbury Cathedral. The Virgin in the vault above the Communion of the Apostles, although of the same date, has been much repainted. In the north recess is a very chilly picture of the Forty Martyrs of Sebaste being frozen to death in an icy pond, and opposite a rather stiff double portrait of Helena and Constantine on either side of the cross. The Last Judgement, which is dated 1333, along with the other paintings in the

narthex, is detailed and enthusiastic; the various departments of Hell are carefully and all too vividly depicted, and the particular tortures reserved for the different categories of sinner are presented with a meticulous realism. It is with some relief that one turns to the very beautiful Panaghia Phorbiotissa in the niche over the door leading into the church, and to a small panel to the right where, for reasons which remain totally unexplained, is a charming little landscape scene of a hound tied to a tree and in the distance two moufflons on a hillside, one of the very, very, rare occasions in which a Byzantine artist has given us what would seem to be the fruit of his own personal observation. In the central bay of the church itself, the paintings are a 14th-century reworking of earlier originals to which the rather hard, dark outlines and strong colour give a slightly *folklorique* air. However, the figure of a saint from which a fragment of the over-painting has flaked away, revealing the original contours, shows that these were followed with considerable fidelity. In a lunette over the south door the church's founder, Nicephorus Magistros, wearing the elaborate uniform of a high Byzantine official, is presenting the church to Christ and the Virgin. An adjacent inscription relates that this took place in 1105 during the reign of Alexios Comnenos. Immediately behind him stands a mysterious lady in the richest possible costume who is recorded as being deceased but whose connection with the donor is not revealed.

LAGOUDERA

The church of the Panaghia tou Arakou is a single-aisled building, domed, with deep arched recesses on the north and south and covered with the usual overall roof resting on carved beams supported by posts and enclosed with trellis work. Inside, the paintings, commissioned by a certain Lord Leon at the very end of the 12th century, form, perhaps, the most complete and consistent series in the island. They represent the court style of the period at its highest point of development and are characterised by an exceptional refinement. Occasionally, as in the scene of the Virgin's presentation in the Temple, with its unnaturally tall and elegant figures and elaborate architectural background, stylisation borders on mannerism, but is everywhere softened by a humanistic Neo-Hellenism which is occasionally carried so far, as in the heads of the two angels in the Baptism, as almost to suggest the hand of the late Lord Leighton. In the dome is a most beautiful and compassionate Pantokrator, as far removed as possible from the gaunt and awe-inspiring image at Daphni, and, in the half-dome of the apse, and very difficult to see, a splendid seated Virgin and Child between archangels. But most beautiful of all is the depiction, in the south recess, of one of the rarest and most moving scenes in the whole of Byzantine iconography—the Dreadful Presentation—where two archangels show to the Christ Child, withdrawn in his Mother's arms, the symbols of the Passion. Elsewhere in the church, of which the walls are completely covered, are many admirable portrait heads, of which the most noteworthy are, perhaps, those of St. Joseph the hymn-writer and St. Lazarus.

GALATA

S. Sozomenus. This, the principal church of the village, has a single-vaulted aisle covered by a pitched roof, and is surrounded on the outside by a wooden trellis reaching up to the eaves. Unlike so many of the Troodos churches it was not the foundation of a local magnate, but was erected by the villagers in the year 1513, when it was decorated by a local painter, Symeon Axenti by name. His style, although slightly rustic by comparison with that of the earlier centuries, owes little or nothing to either the Cretan or Macedonian schools and is rather less provincial in its effect than the contemporary work on the mainland. The upper part of the south wall is covered with scenes from the life of Christ, and on the north is a very full cycle from the Apocryphal life of the Virgin, including the rare incident of the Drinking of the Waters of Conviction. Alongside is a charming Dormition with all the apostles arriving on little clouds, each guided by an attendant angel; above is the Assumption of the Virgin. On the lowest part of the walls are displayed the saints, of whom the most memorable are a very spirited St. George on the north-west, spearing the dragon round whose neck the princess has already got her lead, with scenes from his martyrdom above, and, opposite, a fine St. Mammas astride his lion. On the outside of the north wall are panels showing the great Church Councils, each presided over by an Emperor surrounded by attend-ant bishops and patriarchs, all neatly labelled, while beneath their feet the appropriate heresiarchs disconsolately grovel.

The Panaghia Theotokos. Single-aisled and timber-roofed, this was the founda-tion of a family named Zacharia who all appear in a charming group on the north wall, dated 1514 and signed by Axenti; the men, headed by Paul Zacharia offering a model of the chapel, together with the keys, to Christ, are on the left and the women on the right. Between them is a shield bearing the Zacharia coat of arms impaled, on the distaff side, by those of Lusignan, which possibly explains the extreme richness and western cut of the ladies' clothes. The rest of the wall space is covered by the full liturgical cycle, which includes such Old Testament scenes as the sacrifice of Isaac, and Abraham entertaining the Three Angels. They are well preserved and of a surprisingly high quality for the period. (Axenti would seem to have learnt a lot since the decoration of St. Sozomenus or, perhaps, his rich patrons were more demanding than the villagers.)

The Panaghia Prodithou. Once attached to a vanished monastery, this church was built by another local magnate, whose portrait duly appears offering it to the Virgin, at the very begnniing of the 16th century. Architecturally it resembles the two other churches, but the decoration is very different. The artist responsible, clearly a far more cosmopolitan type than Axenti, was, it is clear from his modelling alone, by no means unaware of contemporary developments in Western painting. His masterpiece is the Virgin enthroned, with the Child upright on her lap, a favourite pose in Cyprus, between arch-angels in the conch of the apse; glorious in colour and beautifully composed, this is one of the best paintings on the island, certainly the best of this period. Opposite, on the west wall, is a large Crucifixion in which both the Two Thieves and the dicing soldiers, whose appearance is very rare in Byzantine art, are prominent. The heads of the mourning women, most delicately modelled and touched by a humanism that clearly derives from the West, prompt the reflection on how much more successfully Byzantine artists in Cyprus assimilated Italian influences than did the contemporary icon-painters of Crete. In the series illustrating the story of Joachim and Anna do not overlook the scene where the couple realise that their prayer has been granted and that Anna is with child, where a genuine emotion is most mov-ingly conveyed.

The keys of all three churches are in the keeping of the enthusiastic, know-ledgeable and English-speaking *pappas* of Galata.

8

THE WEST

AT the time of Justinian the Eastern Empire included within its boundaries most of Italy, the whole of North Africa and such far-flung outposts as Sicily and Sardinia, but today there exist, outside Ravenna, surprisingly few buildings to bear witness to the fact. For one thing Imperial rule was comparatively short-lived, and for another many of these territories already possessed a fully developed tradition of architecture when the Greeks arrived. In North Africa almost all the architectural remains that have survived the Arab invasions pre-date Justinian, and the most considerable artistic evidence of the Byzantine presence is the vast quantity of capitals, many of them of the greatest beauty, that came from some long-vanished 6th-century basilica and were subsequently incorporated in the great mosque at Kairouan. Similarly in Italy there are innumerable palaeo-Christian works of art and architecture, but very few which can unhesitatingly be described as Byzantine, and almost none that can safely be attributed to the age of Justinian.

However, if the power of Constantinople found little architectural expression in the West during the period of its greatest expansion, examples of Byzantine influence at a later date are too many to be catalogued at length in a book such as this. During the iconoclastic controversy Western Christendom came out strongly in support of images, and large numbers of Greek artists and craftsmen, their livelihood threatened and their deepest convictions outraged by the Puritan zeal of Leo the Isaurian, came flocking to Rome. Naturally it was in the realm of decoration rather than in architecture proper, with which Rome was already well supplied, that they made their mark, and almost the only building which, it seems to me, can properly be described as Byzantine (and even here the central area is covered with a vault, not a dome) is the chapel of San Zeno attached to the Church of S. Prassede.

In the 9th century, when, for the last time, the Eastern Church was subjected to iconoclast persecution under Leo the Armenian and his immediate successors, the reigning Pontiff was Paschal I, who would appear to have been a man of wide culture, very respectful of the past, devoted to the saints and martyrs and determined to exalt the status of the Mother of God. To underline his theological position he built, or restored, several churches, employing refugee craftsmen from the East, and decorating them in a style that was almost provocatively iconodule, of which S. Maria in Dominica and S. Prassede were the most important. The former was a rebuilding of a much earlier basilica, and the only signs of Eastern influence in the architecture are two additional apses terminating the aisles and the substitution of arched arcades for the original flat architraves. The decoration, however, is markedly Greek in character; for the first time in Rome the enthroned Virgin appears in the half-dome above the central apse, with the Pope himself, adorned with the square halo of the living, kneeling at her feet.

S. Prassede, as built by Paschal, was a straight basilica carefully modelled on much earlier examples, but it has undergone much subsequent reconstruction. It was originally founded to contain the relics of the martyrs, which the Pope had industriously collected from the catacombs, and attached to a monastery of the Greek Rite. In the apse-mosaic, which is clearly directly inspired by that in the church of SS. Cosma e Damiano, dating from 300 years earlier, SS. Praxede and Pudentiana, who had so carefully preserved the remains of their martyred contemporaries, are being introduced into Paradise, both wearing full Byzantine court dress, by SS. Peter and Paul, above a frieze of apostolic sheep advancing towards the Paschal Lamb.

As the supply of relics proved larger than could be conveniently accommodated in the crypt of the main church, a chapel, dedicated to San Zeno, was added on the north. This simple vaulted square is completely Byzantine, both in the aims pursued and the effect produced. In the vault four angels spring from the four corners and, covering the groins, support with outstretched arms a central medallion of the Pantokrator, a scheme which almost exactly follows that adopted in the 6th century to cover a similar vault in the Archiepiscopal chapel in Ravenna, although there the Pantokrator is missing and the intervening spaces are occupied by the Evangelistic symbols. On the side walls are portraits of saints including SS. Peter and Paul on either side of the Hetoimasia, and the remains of a Transfiguration. Both on the walls and in the vault the background is of glittering, unbroken gold.

It was formerly believed that all these decorations were carried out by local mosaicists, Greek trained and possibly under Greek direction, but it is now thought that they are undoubtedly the work of refugee Greeks. If this is indeed the case, it seems to me that either they had not been in the top class at home, or, which is possibly more likely, that to satisfy the antiquarian enthusiasm of their patron, they were forced deliberately to archaise and adopt a style which had long since become out of date in the East; for it is undeniable that the figures, particularly in the two apses of the main church, are characterised by a strange stiffness and disposed with a notable lack of any underlying rhythm.

Another Roman church dating from the iconoclastic period which is sometimes classed as Byzantine, S. Maria Antiqua, is a remodelled classical building with no Byzantine architectural features whatever. The paintings, however, which were only uncovered at the beginning of the present century and are already badly faded, include portraits of a large number of Orthodox saints, of no great aesthetic importance, many labelled in Greek and bearing some stylistic resemblance to works in that Syrian style which had developed in Cappadocia, and it is clear that the church had strong Greek connections.

Elsewhere in Italy, particularly in those southern regions where Greek remained the common tongue almost to our own day, there exist a number of small Byzantine churches, many of them domed cross-in-squares but few, one gathers, achieving more than a provincial importance. In Sardinia, however, there is one unquestionably Byzantine church of considerable distinction. S. Saturnino in Caligari, much bombed during the war but admirably restored, when later additions were removed, is a domed cruciform with aisles and apsidal transepts. The proportions are impressive, the dome rests on pendentives, and the quality of the stonework is high; none of the original decoration remains, but it seems safe to assume that the church dates from the early 8th century before the coming of the Arabs.

There remains the extraordinary phenomenon of Sicily. Although the island had witnessed exactly the same succession of events as Cyprus and Crete—a longish period of Byzantine rule, a temporary Arab domination and final absorption into a Frankish realm—the cultural outcome was markedly different. Whereas in the other two islands the local architecture remained basically Byzantine, influenced not at all by Islamic art and only in matters of detail by Western, in Sicily the styles of all three nations, Greeks, Arabs, Franks, interacted to produce, finally, an architecture which, if it always remained a mechanical mixture and never quite became a chemical compound, was certainly no longer Byzantine.

In a very large measure this was due to the remarkable Norman family who possessed themselves of the island late in the 11th century. During the whole period of their rule the Hautevilles displayed a religious tolerance and a freedom from racial prejudice, in spectacular contrast to the attitude of their brutish kinsmen at the other end of the Mediterranean, and maintained an enlightened and enthusiastic patronage of the arts unmatched by any other European dynasty until the Renaissance. All the buildings they erected were the outcome of international co-operation, with the result that Gothic arches, Cufic lettering, Greek mosaics, Romanesque plans and Saracenic honeycombs are all frequently to be found side by side in the same structure. The Byzantine contribution to the amalgam was largely confined to mosaic decoration which was applied with equally happy results to a straight-forward Romanesque basilica, such as Cefalu, and to an Arabo-Gothic palace chapel. Architecturally, however, there is only one of these churches that can, by the wildest stretch of imagination, be classified as Byzantine.

The Martorana, or S. Mary's of the Admiral in Palermo, was built in the middle of the 12th century by George of Antioch, a devout man of mixed Greek and Syrian parentage, who, after serving the Arab rulers of Tunis, became the High Admiral of Sicily. In plan it conformed to the established domed cross-in-square of the Middle Byzantine period, with a dome supported on four pillars and with three projecting apses, a narthex and an exo-narthex. Unfortunately, it suffered severe alterations at various periods; in the 16th century the narthex and exo-narthex were incorporated into the nave, in the 17th century the west front was covered by a Baroque façade, while in the 18th the central apse was replaced by a square-ended chancel which was again replaced, in what it was hoped was the original style, in the 19th. However, even in its first state, although basically Byzantine in plan and construction, it was characterised by certain divergencies from the contemporary norm; the dome does not rest on pendentives but on a series of super-imposed squinches, reducing the square, first to an octagon, then to a circle, of an unusual design peculiar to Sicily, and probably Islamic in origin, while the barrel vault over the nave, itself pointed, is supported on markedly stilted Gothic arches.

No alien influences, however, are detectable in the mosaics which conform exactly to the highest standards of Middle Byzantine art. In the dome is the seated Pantokrator surrounded by four angels, whose folded wings form a delightful encirclement, but whose extraordinary attitudes, half crouching, half bowing, produce a slight feeling of unease; below, in the drum, are the prophets, separated from the cupola by an encompassing band inscribed in Cufic lettering with the Arabic translation of a Greek hymn. The Four Evangelists are in the squinches, the Annunciation and the Presentation fill the spandrels of the central arches, and elsewhere are most of the usual cycle and many of the saints; but the Panaghia, who must once have occupied the apse, vanished during the rebuilding. Two portraits survive, although not in their original positions; one of King Roger being crowned by Christ, the other of the Admiral himself doing reverence to the Virgin.

The workmen responsible were certainly Greek, and probably the same as those engaged at Cefalu and the Cappella Palatina, but whereas the work at the former is characterised by a certain hieratic gravity, and at the latter by a greater richness and variety, the Martorana mosaics achieve an unmatched consistency and display a wonderful and far subtler sense of colour. Whether or not you agree with Dr. Demus, who claims for them 'the most perfect charm that can be found in any surviving medieval decoration on Italian soil', it must be admitted that they undoubtedly represent the high water mark of Comnenian mosaic decoration.

While the Byzantine influence on architecture extended eastward well beyond the furthest frontier of the Empire, for all practical purposes Sardinia and Sicily marked the limit of its western expansion. It has, indeed, been claimed that a whole group of churches in south-western France should rightly be included in any catalogue of the Byzantine achievement; but none which I have seen affords much support for this contention. Churches such as Souillac, Cahors and Saintes appear to me to be the work of conventional Romanesque architects who chose to employ the dome; neither the proportions, the plan, nor the decoration in any way conform to the Byzantine pattern, and if the use of the dome was ultimately the result of Greek example, it would seem likely that it was transmitted at second-hand from Cyprus. The one possible exception is the Cathedral of S. Front at Périgueux where the layout is very similar to that of S. Marco at Venice.

There is, however, one building in Northern France in which Byzantine influence is dramatically apparent. The little church at Germigny-des-Prés on the Loire, the oldest in France, was built, it is reliably recorded, in A.D. 806. The plan is a fully developed cross-in-square with apsidal arms to the cross; those on the north, east and south are still standing, that on the west was destroyed in the 12th century to make way for the long Romanesque nave. Over the crossing, formed by intersecting barrel vaults, rises a square tower in three stages, the lowest of which is pierced on all four sides by elegant

little three-arched arcades giving on to the interior of the church; that immediately above it by four windows, of which the flanking strip-pilasters are
markedly Carolingian in style; while the topmost is brought to a circle by

true pendentives supporting a drumless dome invisible without. The angle
chambers are groin-vaulted at a lower level than the *naos* and transepts, and
those on the east were formerly provided with their own absidioles flanking
the main apse externally. The free-standing arches are slightly horse-shoe

shaped, a fact which Strygowski attributes, inevitably, to Armenian influence; others more plausibly to Visigothic. In any case so slight is the deviation from the norm as to be almost imperceptible to the casual visitor.

The most extraordinary feature of all, however, is the mosaic in the half-dome of the apse; here two familiar archangels bend over what appears to be a square chest, itself decorated with two miniature archangels in gold, which may possibly represent the Ark of the Covenant. The workmanship is of high quality and the materials, as has been proved by an analysis of the composition of the tesserae, are Greek. It would seem indisputable, therefore, that the craftsmen responsible were also Greek, and, as the founder of the church, the Bishop of Orléans, was a close friend of Charlemagne, they may well have been some of those whom it is known that the great Emperor brought over from Byzantium to decorate his cathedral at Aachen.

Unfortunately, the church underwent an all too thorough and not very sensitive restoration in the last century, when all the fittings and marble revetments, of which, apparently, a quantity remained in situ, were ruthlessly flung out and the side apses pulled down.

But perhaps the strangest thing about this charming little building, rising so exotically alongside the green water-meadows of the Loire, remains its date. Here is, or was before restoration, a perfect example of the fully developed cross-in-square plan which antedates by nearly a century any still existing in the Byzantine Empire itself. Exactly how and why this came about seems likely to remain one of those fascinating mysteries in which architectural history so fortunately abounds.

GLOSSARY & INDEX

GLOSSARY

AMBO	Pulpit.
ANARGYROI	The healing saints, such as SS. Cosmas and Damian.
ANASTASIS	The Resurrection, symbolised by Christ trampling on the doors of hell.
ASOMATOI	Angels (The Bodiless Ones).
BEMA	Chancel.
DIAKONIKON	A small room flanking the main apse on the north, used as a vestry.
EPITAPHIOS	The body of Our Lord laid on the bier.
EXEDRA	A deep niche, usually semi-circular.
HAGIOS	Saint.
HETOIMASIA	The preparation of the Throne for Judgement Day, a favourite motif in early Byzantine art.
HOSIOS	Blessed.
ICONOSTASIS	The screen, enriched with ikons, dividing the *naos* from the *bema*.
MANDORLA	An all-enclosing glory or halo usually almond-shaped.
NAOS	Nave.
NARTHEX	A porch or vestibule on the west end of the church, originally for the accommodation of the unbaptised.
EXO-NARTHEX	An additional porch, further to the west, sometimes taking the form of a loggia.
OPUS ALEXANDRINUM	Decorative paving.
PANTOKRATOR	Christ the Ruler of all things, usually a half-figure in the central dome.
PAMMAKARISTOS	All-blessed, an epithet applied to the Panaghia.
PANAGHIA	The All Holy Virgin.

177

GLOSSARY

PAREKKLESION   A small additional church or chapel usually attached to an outer wall of the main building.

PRODROMOS   The Forerunner, St. John the Baptist.

PROTHESIS   A small room flanking the main apse on the south used for the preparation of the Elements.

SOLEA   A ramp which in some early churches led from the *bema* to the *ambo*.

SYNTHRONON   A half-circle of seats in the main apse to the east of the Holy Table.

TAXIARCH   Archangel

TEMPLUM   A stone screen separating the *naos* and the *bema*, which became in later times the *iconostasis*.

TESSERAE   The small glass or stone cubes of which a mosaic is built up.

THEOTOKOS   The Mother of God.

INDEX